THE PREACHER HAS IT WRONG

When the Blind Lead the Blind

By *C. Ed Smith*

ISBN 9780615704067

Printed in the United States and Europe

FORWARD

"As we have said before, so say I now again, if any man preacheth unto you any gospel other than that which ye received, let him be anathema," (Gal. 1:9 ASV). The apostle Paul makes it clear: just because a preacher preaches something, that does not make his message correct. Preaching must be examined in the light of Holy Writ. If it disagrees with Scripture, it is wrong! Every time we disagree with the Lord, we are wrong!

In our day and time so many people have fallen into the trap of accepting the word of a preacher instead of "examining the scriptures daily, whether these things were so," (Acts 17:11 ASV). The people of Berea were "noble" because they checked the apostle's preaching to be certain it was scriptural. This enabled them to "receive the word with all readiness of mind." This is the premise of C. Ed Smith's book, *The preacher Has It Wrong: When the Blind Lead the Blind.*

Ed Smith's book will be a tremendous help to at least three groups of people: (1) members of denominational churches who have never examined their preacher's teaching by comparing it with the Bible, God's word; (2) people who have been "turned off" by the religious divisions resulting from un-examined preaching; (3) genuine believers who are not familiar with some of the more popular religious notions espoused by denominational preachers.

This author, Ed Smith, is as common as his name ... and this is a genuine compliment! His education and training surpass mine, but he has never made me feel anything but comfortable when around him ... especially when discussing the word of God. He has served his Lord and Savior through the years as a preacher of the gospel ... sometimes devoting all his time while being supported financially by his hearers, and most often while "making tents" as a school teacher while preaching for small congregations. Due to multiple surgeries on his spine (and extreme pain) he has been limited physically in recent years, but is still capable of teaching God's word via the printed message. To God be the glory!

May God bless Ed with many more years of faithful service. You will be blessed by reading this book and examining it in the light of God's word

Ronnie Henderson

PREFACE

The motivation for writing this book is the sad condition in which we find the so-called Christian world today. The theme, as the title suggests, has to do with the typical denominational preacher who, far too often, disputes what the Bible says. My purpose is to point out some of the most prevalent doctrines taught today that are simply false.

A more important purpose, though, is to help those who have given up on religion because of the vast array of beliefs and teachings that are opposed to each other and to the Bible. While writing this book it has occurred to me how simple it is to arrive at the truth regarding any Bible topic if we just take what the Bible says and leave out our opinions.

A great deal of effort went into being certain the scriptures say what I understand them to say. It will be a challenge for anyone to prove anything they find in this book wrong, because every statement is backed up by scripture.

I'm excited about the potential for anyone who reads the whole book to truly benefit. I expect it to change the lives of those who have given up on religion. So I encourage the reader to read all of the material contained herein.

Read with an open mind and you will find that <u>The Preacher Has it Wrong</u>. You will also find what you really need to do to be saved.

ACKNOWLEDGEMENT

Without the influence of my parents and grandmother, chances are that I would be just like the Gentiles in the Apostle Paul's day. Paul said to the Ephesians Gentiles, "That at that time ye were without Christ, being aliens from the commonwealth of Israel, and strangers from the covenants of promise, having no hope, and without God in the world" (Eph 2:12). I will be eternally grateful to my mom, dad, and grandmother; and to my wife, of nearly fifty years, who has been extremely supportive of me, not just in writing this book, but in all the ups and downs in life over such a long time.

TABLE OF CONTENTS

Introduction   Page 1

The Importance of Doctrine   Page 4

Necessity of Obedience   Page 15

The Importance of the Church   Page 25

The Kingdom   Page 30

Are the Jews Special Today   Page 38

Calvinism -- Part One   Page 47

Calvinism -- Part Two   Page 52

Calvinism -- Part Three   Page 58

The Holy Spirit -- Baptism, Indwelling

    and Miracles   Page 68

What Happens at the Second Coming

    Of Christ   Page 86

Church Organization   Page 103

Admission to the Church and Salvation   Page 109

Importance of the Gospel   Page 117

INTRODUCTION

"And ye shall know the truth, and the truth shall make you free" (John 8:32). Wouldn't it be nice to be set free from the confusion, uncertainty and the objectionable teachings and the obnoxious ranting of the preacher who stands before us with his forced tears? The preacher will find the content of this book offensive. False teachers have always found truth offensive; they did even in Jesus' day.

This is a summary of many things that are wrong in organized religion, things that are taught and practiced under the umbrella of "Christianity." There is so much confusion in religion that the uninformed may just throw up his hands and give up on Jesus altogether. The Bible says that God is not the author of confusion. And Jesus prayed that we all may be one so the world might believe.

For one who is honest, the contents of this book will change his life. And he will find it refreshing. It is important to approach Bible study without preconceived ideas or notions. If one takes the Bible for what it says, and nothing more, it's not hard to arrive at what God expects of us.

Can two differ and both be right? One says the earth is flat, another says the earth is round; one is wrong. One says two plus two is five, another says two plus two is six; both are wrong. There are hundreds of different kinds of churches, each teaching something different from all others. Can they all be right? Can more than one be right? Many, if not all, teach things that are completely opposite from others. Facts are facts in science, history or math, but not so in regards to the Bible, according to the preacher.

1

Jesus said many will think they had done His will but will be rejected and lost. "Many will say to me in that day, Lord, Lord, have we not prophesied in thy name? and in thy name have cast out devils? and in thy name done many wonderful works? And then will I profess unto them, I never knew you: depart from me, ye that work iniquity" (Matt. 7:22-23). Jesus also said, "Enter ye in at the strait gate: for wide *is* the gate, and broad *is* the way, that leadeth to destruction, and many there be which go in thereat: Because strait *is* the gate, and narrow *is* the way, which leadeth unto life, and few there be that find it" (Matt. 7:13-14). It looks like Jesus said only a few would be saved. It certainly shows that most will be wrong.

Two words come to mind when thinking of what men have done to the scriptures: "indecent" and "offensive"? It's worse. "It *is* a fearful thing to fall into the hands of the living God" (Heb. 10:31).

The preacher, far too often, has it wrong. The Bible gives numerous warnings about false teachers. If there were false teachers in the days the Bible was written, why should we think there are no false teachers today? It doesn't matter what anyone says or what anyone feels, if it doesn't agree with the Bible it's wrong.

Every Sunday the preacher stands in the pulpit and too often what he says is just insidious. Something insidious, by definition, is dangerous because it seems to be harmless or not important but, in fact, causes harm. If the preacher cannot show scripture for what he says, there is something terribly wrong. If he preaches something opposite of what another preacher preaches, one of them is wrong. This cannot be denied. It's appalling and indefensible what religious leaders are doing and saying, and claiming it's "in the name of the Lord."

2

It didn't take long after the apostles died, for Christianity to begin evolving into what we know today. But all through the centuries it has been possible (sadly, sometimes at the risk of torture or death) to obey God. The attempt here is to identify some of the most prominent false doctrines taught today and to show why they are false.

In almost all cases the scripture references are printed out so you will not have to look them up. Please check your Bible if you are in doubt. The words in italics are in italics in the Bible. The King James Version is used almost exclusively throughout.

As you read you must decide if you will serve the Lord and be saved, or will you hold onto your friends, family, and a church started by men; and will you hold onto the traditions of men. If you are interested in only the social aspects of church life, any church will do.

THE IMPORTANCE OF DOCTRINE

There are hundreds of different kinds of churches in America. The question is, "Why?" Another question is, "Is it good that there are so many different churches?" Many would say yes, because surely of all the variety of churches, everyone should be able to find one that pleases him. WWJD? Maybe it should be WWJS (what would Jesus say)? What do you think Jesus would say? What would He say about all the religious division, about doctrine, about the Holy Spirit, about miracles, and what would Jesus say about how one becomes a Christian? Church leaders give an array of answers to these important questions. Most church leaders and preachers are wrong, and if you keep reading you will agree.

The preacher says that it doesn't matter what you believe just so long as you believe. Of course, they say that you have to believe in Jesus, but beyond that it just doesn't matter. This is very convenient but not true. Where do you suppose the idea came from? Is it possible that church leaders want to make it easy so they can draw in more adherents to their fellowship? More people means more popularity for the preacher. More people means more money. To avoid appearing cynical and without judging, probably some church leaders really do think that it doesn't matter what one believes so long as he has faith in Jesus.

Do leaders of today know more than Jesus and the divinely inspired apostles? If so, then it is okay to accept the idea that it doesn't matter what one believes. If not so, then it becomes paramount that we learn just what Jesus and the apostles had to say about what we believe.

Jesus said, "Many will say to me in that day, Lord, Lord, have we not prophesied in thy name? and in thy name

4

have cast out devils? and in thy name done many wonderful works? And then will I profess unto them, I never knew you: depart from me, ye that work iniquity" (Matt 7:22-23). Jesus had to be talking about people who had faith and thought they were pleasing Him in their religious practices and teachings. How terrible to face Him on judgment day and hear those words! Back in verse 15, He warned, "Beware of false prophets."

Some will say the Bible is too complicated. They will insist that it's too complicated for us to understand and certainly too complicated for us all to understand it the same way. But, in fact, it's not. We might complicate it by what we do to it. We can all understand, and we can understand it alike. Jesus said, "Ask, and it shall be given you; seek, and ye shall find; knock, and it shall be opened unto you" (Matt 7:7). It does take effort to arrive at the truth. We do have to seek. And after considering the warning of Jesus we'd better put some effort into learning what God expects of us.

To the scribes and Pharisees who were questioning Jesus about why His disciples were not washing their hands before eating, according to the traditions of the elders, Jesus said, "This people honoureth me with *their* lips, but their heart is far from me. Howbeit in vain do they worship me, teaching *for* doctrines the commandments of men. For laying aside the commandment of God, ye hold the tradition of men" (Mark 7:6-8). Are the traditions of men acceptable? Surely not! Is, then, what we believe and practice important? Of course, it is. So, is doctrine important?

In regards to traditions of men the Apostle Paul wrote, "Beware lest any man spoil you through philosophy and vain deceit, after the tradition of men" (Col 2:8). It has always been God's will that no one add to or take from

5

His Word. Even back in the Old Testament it was condemned. Read Deut 12:32, "What thing soever I command you, observe to do it: thou shalt not add thereto, nor diminish from it." It's frightening to think that church leaders say it doesn't matter. In I Timothy, Paul told Timothy to "charge some that they teach no other doctrine" (1 Tim 1:3).

The Apostle Peter taught, "If any man speak, *let him speak* as the oracles of God. . . (1 Peter 4:11) Common sense should tell us that we should not add to or take from God's Word. But in spite of what the Bible says many still do add to and take from it. The Apostle John offered an ominous warning, "Whosoever transgresseth, and abideth not in the doctrine of Christ, hath not God. He that abideth in the doctrine of Christ, he hath both the Father and the Son" (2 John 1:9).

Let's suppose that two men, John and Bill, decide to do some Bible teaching in different places. John goes to Orlando and Bill goes to Atlanta. Each takes with him only the Bible. When they arrive in their respective cities, they begin teaching. Since the Bible says that there is no private interpretation of the scripture (II Peter 1:20), they teach just what it says, nothing more, and nothing less. When people hear their teaching and believe, if they accept the teaching and are converted, what are they? What are they called? Are they Baptists? Are the Catholics? Are they Methodists? Are they members of any denomination? In Acts chapter 2, verse 47, Luke, the writer of the Book of Acts, said, "the Lord added to the church daily such as should be saved." Since the converts in Atlanta and Orlando heard the same message and obeyed the teachings of that message they are Christians, nothing more and nothing less. They are members of the Lord's church, for He added them to His church. They didn't then go out and join any

6

denomination, because there is nothing about denominations in that message they heard. The people in Acts chapter two certainly didn't join a denomination for they didn't exist in Bible times.

Consider the fact that you cannot learn how to be a Catholic, a Baptist, a Methodist, or a member of any other denomination from the Bible! This should alert us to the possibility that two opposing doctrines cannot both be right. If it doesn't matter what we believe they can both be right. Of course, this is not so in math or science or history. It is not so in any other field of study. But church leaders teach that it is so in religion and in regards to the Bible. They teach that it doesn't matter whether you are a Baptist, a Catholic, or a member of any other denomination. Now, some may draw the line with accepting the Mormon doctrine. But why? The Mormons have done nothing different from other denominations; they just did more of it. They added another whole book. But if one person can add a little another person can add a lot.

What's the difference between adding another book like the Book of Mormon from adding a book called a church creed, for example, the Baptist Manual? The Baptist Manual is a book. Any church creed besides the Bible is an addition to the Bible, whether it's Baptist, Presbyterian, Methodist, or whatever. The Book of Mormon is what Mormons believe. The creed book of any church is what that church believes. What's the difference? No human creed is okay! If it is shorter than the Bible it's too short. If it's longer than the Bible it's too long. If it's the same as the Bible it's not necessary; we have the Bible. Besides, by whose authority do men write creeds? It's certainly not by God's authority that men write creeds. God condemns such as we have already seen.

Jesus said, "Beware of false prophets" (Matt 7:15). Hebrews 13:9 warns, "Be not carried about with divers and strange doctrines" But who is a false prophet? It's surely not the man who stands in the pulpit every Sunday morning and admonishes the flock to follow good works. Yes, it could be that very man, or it could be a loving and caring parent or grandparent. It doesn't necessarily mean that the false teacher is a bad person. Good people can be misguided. And with several centuries of religious evolution, with the devil doing all he can to deceive, no one should be surprised that false doctrines have been developed and taught.

Suppose one's loving grandparent or parent died believing and practicing a false doctrine. Would that person want the grandchild or child to follow in his or her steps? If the child does not follow the parent or grandparent, is he or she condemning the parent or grandparent to hell? No. It's foolish to take the risk of following a misguided parent, grandparent, or preacher. Each will answer for himself. God does the judging. Some people seem to think that if they abandon their dead parent's religion to accept the truth that they are judging that parent to hell. What they do does not change the condition of the loving parent or grandparent.

It doesn't matter who the misguided teacher is, it's so important that we learn the truth. Too much is at stake. Consider these words of Jesus, "He that loveth father or mother more than me is not worthy of me: and he that loveth son or daughter more than me is not worthy of me" (Matt 10:37). We must love Jesus more. And just because someone else is wrong doesn't mean we should be, especially if it means we will be lost eternally.

Think how wonderful that He, "According as his divine power hath given unto us all things that *pertain* unto life and godliness, through the knowledge of him that hath called us to glory and virtue: Whereby are given unto us exceeding great and precious promises" (2 Peter 1:3-4). This passage tells us that through His Word, God has given us everything we need to live this life, and how to be godly. We don't need anything more. Therefore we contend for the faith which is the doctrine. Jude said, "it was needful for me to write unto you, and exhort *you* that ye should earnestly contend for the faith which was once delivered unto the saints" (Jude 1:3). So, the doctrine was delivered once and we should contend for it. Between these two passages we see that we do not need more revelation. God's revelation has been delivered for all time and shall never pass away. Jesus said, "Heaven and earth shall pass away, but my words shall not pass away" (Matt 24:35).

Near the very end of the Bible John wrote, "For I testify unto every man that heareth the words of the prophecy of this book, If any man shall add unto these things, God shall add unto him the plagues that are written in this book: And if any man shall take away from the words of the book of this prophecy, God shall take away his part out of the book of life, and out of the holy city, and *from* the things which are written in this book" (Rev 22:18-19). Here John is referring to the Book of Revelation but the principle applies to all of God's Word.

Ponder briefly a few common traditions of men that are different from what the Bible teaches.

One thing that is practiced commonly in several churches and is taught by the preacher is that of baptizing babies. But Jesus said, "He that believeth and is baptized shall be saved" (Mark 16:16). Babies can't believe. But that doesn't matter, because the preacher says baptize him any way. Surely the preacher knows best.

9

Often the preacher says, "Join the church of your choice." That's fine, because the preacher said it! But it's smart first to see who started the church and what it teaches before joining it. Jesus said, "I will build my church" (Matt 16:18). It's okay to join the church of your choice so long as it is the church that Jesus built.

The preacher says it's okay to be called a Baptist, a Methodist or a Presbyterian. In the early days of the church the disciples of Christ were called Christian. "And the disciples were called Christians first in Antioch" (Acts 11:26). It's risky to wear a different name because in Acts 4:12, we learn, "Neither is there salvation in any other: for there is none other name under heaven given among men, whereby we must be saved." Did you know that God prophesied in the Old Testament the name by which we are to be called? We read in Isaiah 62:2. "And the Gentiles shall see thy righteousness, and all kings thy glory: and thou shalt be called by a new name, which the mouth of the LORD shall name." But the preacher will tell you that it's not that important. He'll say there's nothing in a name even though it's a name that God ordained. Dare we wear a man made name?

Some people actually call other men "father." That must be okay, too, because the preacher says so. But Jesus said, "call no *man* your father upon the earth: for one is your Father, which is in heaven" (Matt 23:9). Jesus must not have known better.

Some people refer to their preacher as reverend. However much he may like to be called reverend, or however good it may make him look, it's scary. The preacher is a brave man, taking on himself that which refers to God. Speaking of God the Psalmist said, "holy and reverend *is* his name" (Psalms 111:9). Nowhere in the scriptures is man referred to as reverend. There's no authority for it.

10

The preacher recommends having the Lord's Supper on a week day. But Paul didn't know that was acceptable. In Acts 20:7, "And upon the first *day* of the week, when the disciples came together to break bread," Paul was there with them. It was the first day of the week, and they had gathered for worship. The Lords Supper was the very purpose for which they came together. That's what it says, "<u>to</u> break bread." This and one other place in the Bible tell us why the early Christians came together on the Lord's Day. The other place is 1 Cor 11:20. Paul was trying to correct a problem. They were coming together to have a common meal and He said, "When ye come together therefore into one place, *this* is not to eat the Lord's Supper." Paul was saying you are not coming together <u>to</u> have the Lord's Supper as you should be, instead you are coming together and making a meal for yourselves. If you want to follow Bible example, have the Lord's Supper on the first day of the week only. Historians tell you that the early Christians met for communion on the first day of the week. The preacher shouldn't change that.

The treasury runs low and the preacher says it's time to have a bake sale. Paul didn't know you could do that to raise money. He gave a different kind of instruction: "Upon the first *day* of the week let every one of you lay by him in store, as *God* hath prospered him" (1 Cor 16:2). "Every man according as he purposeth in his heart, *so let him give*; not grudgingly, or of necessity: for God loveth a cheerful giver" (2 Cor 9:7).

Now, is it time to make accusations of judging? No one is judging. Is it judging to tell the truth? Doctrine is extremely important no matter what anyone has to say.

It shouldn't be necessary to point out that the scriptures give us everything we need to know in order to please

God, and that it's a violation of God's will to add to His Word. Notice several passages which tell us that we find in the scriptures <u>all</u> we need to please Him.

Before Jesus went back to heaven, He told His disciples that He would not leave them alone, but that He would send the Holy Spirit. Jesus told them the Holy Spirit would remind them of the things He had taught them, and would show them things to come. Notice particularly the word "all" in this and the following scriptures.

"But the Comforter, *which is* the Holy Ghost, whom the Father will send in my name, he shall teach you all things, and bring all things to your remembrance, whatsoever I have said unto you" (John 14:26). A couple of chapters later, we find Jesus saying, "Howbeit when he, the Spirit of truth, is come, he will guide you into all truth: for he shall not speak of himself; but whatsoever he shall hear, *that* shall he speak: and he will shew you things to come" (John 16:13).

The apostles, who were responsible for delivering the scriptures to us, were told that the Holy Spirit would teach them "all things" and guide them into "all truth." Again, the emphasis is on the word "all."

If the Holy Spirit guided the apostles into <u>all</u> truth, there is no more truth besides that which He delivered. Any teaching coming from man is not truth. It must be false. This is why the scriptures warn us that there will be false teachers. Religious people today seem to think that anyone who claims to preach in the name of Jesus must be righteous no matter how blatantly he may differ from the inspired Word. A teacher cannot differ from the Bible without teaching false doctrine. Two teachers cannot differ from each other without at least one of them teaching false doctrine.

Paul told the Ephesians elders that he had given them all of God's counsel. He said, "For I have not shunned to declare unto you all the counsel of God" (Acts 20:27). God's counsel is what's so desperately needed today.

"Grace and peace be multiplied unto you through the knowledge of God, and of Jesus our Lord, According as his divine power hath given unto us all things that *pertain* unto life and godliness, through the knowledge of him that hath called us to glory and virtue" (2 Peter 1:2-3). Peter said these words as he began his second letter. He stated that God has given us all things that pertain to life and godliness, and what He has given comes through knowledge. Since God has given us all things, there is nothing more! Man has nothing more to offer besides what God has already given. Why should we presume to add to His word or to change it?

When the Apostle Paul was finally put into prison he knew that his life, and his ministry were soon to end. He wrote to his friend, Timothy, and told him, in so many words, that man should not depend on anything but scriptures for their spiritual instruction and for religious authority. He said, "All scripture *is* given by inspiration of God, and *is* profitable for doctrine, for reproof, for correction, for instruction in righteousness: That the man of God may be perfect, throughly furnished unto all good works" (2 Tim 3:16-17). Where the word "perfect" is used here; it is translated "complete," "competent" or "fitted" in newer translations. Inspiration of scriptures indicates that God breathed the scriptures.

"All scripture *is* given by inspiration." Inspiration means God breathed. So God breathed to the apostles those things that completely furnish us with instructions regarding what is "good works." Since the instructions are complete, there are no good works not found in the Bible.

Our faith should come by reading or hearing God's word. "So then faith *cometh* by hearing, and hearing by the word of God" (Romans 10:17). The faith is the body of doctrine which we believe.

"O Lord, I know that the way of man *is* not in himself: *it is* not in man that walketh to direct his steps" (Jer 10:23). If you cannot direct your own steps, do you want some other man to direct them? The preacher has it wrong; he is not a good director. Jesus said, "in vain they do worship me, teaching *for* doctrines the commandments of men" (Matt 15:9).

Jesus and the apostles taught that the scriptures would provide "all truth," "all things that pertain to life and godliness," "all God's counsel" and furnish us with instruction regarding "all good works."

Every church creed or church manual represents a new counsel, the counsel of men. Any new or different counsel or creed has to be something besides God's counsel.

"Beloved, believe not every spirit, but try the spirits whether they are of God: because many false prophets are gone out into the world" (1 John 4:1).

The preacher is wrong. It does matter what we believe.

14

NECESSITY OF OBEDIENCE

The preacher today says that you don't have to do anything to be saved except believe. Is he right? He says it because the Bible teaches that salvation is a gift of God. Salvation is clearly and definitely a gift from God.

So your neighbor, Bill, tells his sixteen-year-old son, Billy, that he will buy him a brand new car if he will only mow the small front yard. Billy mows the yard and gets the car. Is the car a gift or did Billy earn it? Billy could not have gotten the car unless he mowed the yard. Something was required of Billy in order for him to receive the gift. The question is, "Did Billy earn the car for mowing the yard?" Surely Billy did not earn the car. This is how God's grace works. Grace is generally defined as favor not earned. God offers us favor, and, in fact, we cannot earn it. At the same time we cannot receive God's favor unless we do what He tells us to.

As we mature as Christians we obey God not just to receive His favor but because of our love for Him, and because we know it's best for us and that it, at the same time, pleases Him. Jesus said, "If ye love me, keep my commandments" (John 14:15). Our love results from His love for us. He died to save us from our sins.

Look first at just a couple of Old Testament passages to learn God's attitude toward man's obedience. "Now therefore, if ye will obey my voice indeed, and keep my covenant, then ye shall be a peculiar treasure unto me above all people: for all the earth *is* mine" (Ex. 19:5). "Thou shalt therefore obey the voice of the Lord thy God, and do his commandments and his statutes, which I command thee this day" (Deut. 27:10).

15

In prophesying concerning the church (the kingdom of God), Daniel said, "And the kingdom and dominion, and the greatness of the kingdom under the whole heaven, shall be given to the people of the saints of the most High, whose kingdom *is* an everlasting kingdom, and all dominions shall serve and obey him" (Dan. 7:27). Notice here that not just the Jewish nation but all dominions shall obey Him.

This discussion should not be necessary. Common sense tells us that we must obey God. This discussion is necessary because pronouncements come forth from radio, TV and the pulpits constantly that there is nothing we can do to be saved and that obedience is not required; God's grace alone saves us.

Jesus Himself set the example of obedience, "Though he were a Son, yet learned he obedience by the things which he suffered; And being made perfect, he became the author of eternal salvation unto all them that obey him" (Heb. 5:8-9). Notice, salvation is conditional. It depends on our obeying Him. Salvation is for "all them that <u>obey</u> him."

If a brother refuses to obey the Lord, the rest of the church is to avoid him. "And if any man obey not our word by this epistle, note that man, and have no company with him, that he may be ashamed" (2 Thess. 3:14). The context of this passage indicates that Paul is talking about how the church is to deal with one of God's people who refuses to obey God.

At one point there was a problem with the church at Galatia. Some in that church had moved away from the truth. Paul asked, "O foolish Galatians, who hath bewitched you, that ye should not obey the truth" (Gal. 3:1). A little later in the same letter he asked, "Ye did run

16

well; who did hinder you that ye should not obey the truth?" Then Paul explained, "This persuasion *cometh* not of him that calleth you" (Gal. 5:7-8). Their acceptance of false doctrine did not come from Him who had called them; it had not come from God. But someone had come along teaching something different from the truth. What is God's attitude today concerning anyone who would deviate from the doctrine of Christ and therefore not obey it?

Maybe II Thess. 1:7-9 answers that question: "And to you who are troubled rest with us, when the Lord Jesus shall be revealed from heaven with his mighty angels, In flaming fire taking vengeance on them that know not God, and that obey not the gospel of our Lord Jesus Christ: Who shall be punished with everlasting destruction from the presence of the Lord, and from the glory of his power." Is obedience necessary, or are we saved by grace without obedience? What about those who "obey not the gospel?"

Of course, one can deliberately choose not to obey God. Consider Romans 6:16: "Know ye not, that to whom ye yield yourselves servants to obey, his servants ye are to whom ye obey; whether of sin unto death, or of obedience unto righteousness?" If we choose not to obey God, we automatically are obeying "sin unto death." We can serve God. If not, we are servants of Satan!

Again, what about those who do not obey the gospel? Peter asked that very question to emphasize what awaits those who do not obey. "Yet if *any man suffer* as a Christian, let him not be ashamed; but let him glorify God on this behalf. For the time *is come* that judgment must begin at the house of God: and if *it* first *begin* at us, what shall the end *be* of them that obey not the gospel of God? And if the righteous scarcely be saved, where shall the

17

ungodly and the sinner appear?" (1 Peter 4:16-18). What does await those who do not obey the gospel?

What is it to "obey the gospel"? We've been told that the gospel is good news. In this case it is the good news of our salvation through the death and resurrection of Christ. But how do we obey it? Simply put, we obey the gospel by doing what the Bible tells us to do. But Paul in Romans chapter six elaborates more completely the process of conversion and, therefore, what it is to obey the gospel.

"What shall we say then? Shall we continue in sin, that grace may abound? God forbid. How shall we, that are dead to sin, live any longer therein? Know ye not, that so many of us as were baptized into Jesus Christ were baptized into his death? Therefore we are buried with him by baptism into death: that like as Christ was raised up from the dead by the glory of the Father, even so we also should walk in newness of life. For if we have been planted together in the likeness of his death, we shall be also *in the likeness* of *his* resurrection: Knowing this, that our old man is crucified with *him,* that the body of sin might be destroyed, that henceforth we should not serve sin. For he that is dead is freed from sin. Now if we be dead with Christ, we believe that we shall also live with him" (Romans 6:1-8).

In case anyone should think they should sin more in order for God's grace to abound, Paul explained that this is just not what we should do. To emphasize his point he asked, "Shall we continue in sin, that grace may abound?" He followed with "God forbid." Then he asked, "How shall we, that are dead to sin, live any longer therein?" Since death means separation (at least, it does here), the righteous are separated from sin. Of course, the righteous should not continue in sin. In the natural

18

realm death is the separation of the spirit from the body. In this case death (to sin) is the separation of the individual from sin.

We are baptized into Christ thereby we were baptized into His death. It was in His death that His blood was shed. We are saved by the blood of Christ (Romans 5:9). It is in baptism that we receive the benefit of the blood of Christ.

So we, like He was raised from the dead, are also raised from the dead. We were once dead in sin, we die to sin (that is repentance), then we are buried as Jesus was, but our burial is in water. His was in a tomb. Then we are raised from the watery grave of baptism to, as Paul said, walk a new life. Our new life begins then, but not before we are raised from the grave of baptism.

Stated simply, one dies to sin or separates himself from it by quitting sin. This is repentance. This person who dies to sin is buried, like Jesus was (only ours is in water), then we are raised to walk a new life. This burial in water is baptism which meant immersion in water. <u>This is how we obey the gospel.</u>

The only way we get into Christ is by baptism. "For by one Spirit are we all baptized into one body" (1 Cor. 12:13). "For as many of you as have been baptized into Christ have put on Christ" (Gal. 3:27). This is the only way the Bible tells us how to get into Christ. There is no other way to get into Christ; it matters not what the preacher says.

What is a command except something to be obeyed? No one questions that the Jews in the Old Testament were expected to obey the Ten Commandments. All God's commands, He expects to be obeyed. Jesus said regarding what is commanded, "when ye shall have done

19

all those things which are commanded you, say, We are unprofitable servants: we have done that which was our duty to do" (Luke 17:10). It is only reasonable that we obey God; even then we are unprofitable servants.

Those who say there is nothing we have to do to be saved agree that we have to believe or have faith. The Bible calls faith a work, "Remembering without ceasing your work of faith, and labour of love" (1 Thess. 1:3). Besides, James said, "Even so faith, if it hath not works, is dead, being alone" (James 2:17). Further, He said, "Ye see then how that by works a man is justified, and not by faith only" (James 2:24). By the way, this is the only place in the Bible where the phrase "faith only" is used. How many times have you heard misinformed preachers say that we are saved by faith only? Along with faith the works which save are the works which God ordained, not works of our own conjuring, or in this dispensation, not the works of the Old Testament.

We learn in Acts 5:32 that the Holy Ghost is given to those who obey God. Obedience is necessary to receive the Holy Ghost. It is not, as the preacher says, the Holy Ghost has to work on one somehow before He believes. And they say, only then is he even capable of believing. The fact is we believe after hearing the gospel, and it moves us to obey. "How then shall they call on him in whom they have not believed? and how shall they believe in him of whom they have not heard? and how shall they hear without a preacher?" (Romans 10:14). And then we are saved by obeying the gospel. Paul goes on to say in verse 16, "For I am not ashamed of the gospel of Christ: for it is the power of God unto salvation."

Farmer John and his son, Johnny, are going to start farming a new piece of property John just bought. Just as they got started the father, John, got called away.

Before he left he laid out the plans for all of the farm structures including the house. After all, he had paid for the farm so he should have that privilege. So he gave strict instructions and told Johnny how and what to build and where to build each structure. He told Johnny to put the house on the northwest corner, the barn on the northeast corner, the chicken house on the southwest corner, and the well on the southeast corner. So Johnny started building. He put the house where his dad had told him to, as his dad had commanded. He put the chicken house where his dad had told him to, as his dad had commanded. But when he got ready for the barn and well, he decided to switch their locations because if not the surface water from the barn would run into the well.

When Johnny built the house, did he obey his father's command? When he built the chicken house, did he obey his father's command? The answer to both is emphatically No! He just happened to agree with his father, otherwise he would have switched them, too. He happened to agree with his father that the house and the chicken house should be where he put them. He didn't obey his father in building any of these structures.

Preachers do this in regards to God's instructions all the time. They change the parts they don't like. If they can change a little, they can change a lot. Why not just change it all?

Oh! So, some zealous, well meaning young man comes along and says, "Okay, I'm going to do all God says to do and everything else I can in the name of Christ in my practice of Christianity. I'm going to use candles in my services. I'm going to sound a trumpet before and after observing the Lord's Supper. I'm going to not only baptize but also sprinkle everyone who wants to be saved. Let

21

us, in fact, offer cake on the Lords Table." And the list can go on and on.

First of all, this young man cannot do those things "in the name of Christ." For a thing to be done in Christ's name, Christ had to have authorized it. Christ has authorized none of these things. How sad that most people in their religious practices do many things in addition to what God has authorized. They argue that if the Bible is silent on a subject we have the prerogative to do whatever we choose. "The Bible didn't say not to," they will say. But the Apostle Paul said, "And whatsoever ye do in word or deed, *do* all in the name of the Lord" (Col. 3:17). We cannot offer incense before communion, or anything else that God has not authorized and be pleasing to Him, because we cannot do these things "in the name of the Lord" or by His authority.

Notice a passage that is often quoted: "All scripture *is* given by inspiration of God, and *is* profitable for doctrine, for reproof, for correction, for instruction in righteousness: That the man of God may be perfect, throughly furnished unto all good works" (2 Tim. 3:16-17). If in the inspired scriptures we find that which "thoroughly" furnishes us unto "all good works" it seems that there is no good work not found in the scriptures. Other versions do not use the word "perfect" in verse seventeen. Instead they use words like "complete" or "adequate." We do not need the candles to please God. In fact, any addition would be a bad addition since it is not mentioned in scripture. We have been completely, adequately and perfectly supplied with all the instruction we need.

The Apostle Peter told his fellow Christians that our Lord "hath given unto us all things that *pertain* unto life and godliness, through the knowledge of him" (2 Peter 1:3).

22

Any church creed is an addition to the Bible and is, therefore, displeasing to God. He has given us all things that make us godly.

Notice one more passage that deals with this matter of "God didn't say not to." "And these things, brethren, I have in a figure transferred to myself and *to* Apollos for your sakes; that ye might learn in us not to think *of men* above that which is written" (1 Cor. 4:6). Notice that the phrase "of men" is in italics. When the King James Version was translated, certain words were supplied by the translators to make the reading clearer. The words which were added are italicized.

This statement, "not to think *of men* above that which is written" doesn't seem so significant until you read it in other versions of the Bible. The New King James, the English Standard, the American Standard versions, and the Young's Literal Translation all teach in this passage not to go beyond what is written. Are we ready to stand before Jesus at judgment having added to what God told us to do, or having done things in our religious practices that He "didn't say not to" do?

We know that God is pleased when we worship Him as He ordained for Jesus said, "But the hour cometh, and now is, when the true worshippers shall worship the Father in spirit and in truth: for the Father seeketh such to worship him. God *is* a Spirit: and they that worship him must worship *him* in spirit and in truth" (John 4:23-24).

To worship "in spirit" suggests to worship with the right attitude. To worship "in truth" is to worship according to truth.

"Whosoever transgresseth, and abideth not in the doctrine of Christ, hath not God. He that abideth in the

23

doctrine of Christ, he hath both the Father and the Son" (2 John 1:9).

Without question, we are saved by the grace of God, but obedience is also necessary. And it's important that we not go beyond what is written.

The preacher has it wrong.

THE IMPORTANCE OF THE CHURCH

Many people believe the church is not essential, (therefore, not all that important) just so long as you accept Jesus into your heart. In fact, many church leaders and preachers believe and teach that you can be saved without having anything to do with the church. But what does the Bible say? Does it even matter? Does it matter that <u>Jesus died for the church</u>? "Christ also loved the church, and gave himself for it" (Eph. 5:25). Since Jesus gave Himself on the cross for the church it must be pretty important. Besides, Acts 2:47 says "And the Lord added to the church daily such as should be saved." (By the way, that phrase "accept Jesus into your heart" is not in the Bible; and the idea is nowhere taught in the Bible.)

It is helpful to first take a look at some of the things the Bible calls the church. This organization consisting of Christians is quite often referred to just as "the church." The word "church" comes from an original Greek word which meant the "called out." In this case, people are called out of the world to serve Christ and to be His disciples. Some of the words or phrases that refer to the church are as follows:

Body -- "And hath put all *things* under his feet, and gave him *to be* the head over all *things* to the church, Which is his body, the fulness of him that filleth all in all." (Eph. 1:22-23)

House of God -- "But if I tarry long, that thou mayest know how thou oughtest to behave thyself in the house of God, which is the church of the living God, the pillar and ground of the truth." (1 Tim. 3:15)

Temple -- "In whom all the building fitly framed together groweth unto an holy temple in the Lord:" (Eph. 2:21)

Kingdom -- "Who hath delivered us from the power of darkness, and hath translated *us* into the kingdom of his dear Son:" (Col. 1:13)

Church of God -- "Unto the church of God which is at Corinth, to them that are sanctified in Christ Jesus, called *to be* saints, with all that in every place call upon the name of Jesus Christ our Lord, both theirs and ours:" (1 Cor. 1:2)

Church of Christ -- "Salute one another with an holy kiss. The churches of Christ salute you." (Romans 16:16)

Actually, it appears that the church does not have a name. These are all descriptive terms or phrases. These terms and phrases describe the organization consisting of Christians. It is the organization to which the Lord adds one when he or she is saved. "And the Lord added to the church daily such as should be saved" (Acts 2:47).

Focus for a while on the term "body". The church is the body of Christ. That is exactly what Ephesians 1:22-23 says, as we just read. When we look further concerning the body, we learn that there is only one body. Speaking of the church, the Apostle Paul said, "But now *are they* many members, yet but one body" (1 Cor. 12:20). One Bible reference to the "one body" should be enough. But there are more. Consider Colossians 3:15: "And let the peace of God rule in your hearts, to the which also ye are called in one body." The significance is that if there is only one body, since the body is the church, there must be only one church.

26

In spite of the preacher's opinion, the church is extremely important and being in the church is <u>essential to our salvation</u> since the saved are added to it. "Christ is the head of the church: and he is the saviour of the body" (Eph. 5:23). The Bible says nothing about anyone being saved outside of the church, the body of Christ.

All this may cause one to ask, though he is attending a church, "whose church am I attending? Is it some church started by men since New Testament times? Or is it the Lord's church?" Jesus said to Peter that upon the fact that He was the Son of God, as stated by Peter, He would build His church. "And I say also unto thee, That thou art Peter, and upon this rock I will build my church; and the gates of hell shall not prevail against it" (Matt. 16:18). The rock was not Peter, as Catholics teach, but it was the fact as stated by Peter that Jesus was the Son of God. All who are serious about pleasing God and being saved will want to be a part of the church which Jesus built. By definition, the word "Peter" meant pebble. And by definition, the word "rock" on which Jesus would build His church meant boulder. So the church was not built on Peter. Peter held no higher position in the church than any other apostle, not withstanding Catholic teaching.

"Except the Lord build the house, they labour in vain that build it" (Psalms 127:1). Who is bold enough to start a church and claim that man can be saved as part of it? Who can be foolish enough?

Could God possibly be pleased with all the division in religion? Notice the prayer Jesus prayed in John 17:21. He prayed that His disciple be united so the world would believe. It's not hard to understand why the world does not believe with all the confusion in religion. "That they all may be one; as thou, Father, *art* in me, and I in thee, that they also may be one in us: that the world may believe that thou hast sent me" (John 17:21).

It's not judging to tell the truth. The truth is, hundreds of churches have been started by men. But by whose authority have all these churches been started? Certainly not by the authority of Christ. For one thing, "God is not the author of confusion" (ICor.14:33). And it's extremely confusing when one church teaches one thing and another teaches something diametrically opposed, something completely opposite. One or the other has to be wrong; possibly both are wrong!

The very word "denomination" suggests division. The disciples of Jesus thought the Pharisees might have been offended at some of Jesus' teaching. He said, "Every plant, which my heavenly Father hath not planted, shall be rooted up. Let them alone: they be blind leaders of the blind. And if the blind lead the blind, both shall fall into the ditch" (Matt. 15:13-14). Was Jesus being judgmental, or was He just telling the truth? Do we judge today when we tell the truth? What was Jesus talking about? Could it be churches started by man? Consider this, what could that plant be today but churches which the "heavenly Father hath not planted?"

The Apostle Paul said, "Now I beseech you, brethren, by the name of our Lord Jesus Christ, that ye all speak the same thing, and *that* there be no divisions among you; but *that* ye be perfectly joined together in the same mind and in the same judgment" (1 Cor. 1:10).

The church is essential. And that makes it all the more important that we seek it out and be part of it, especially considering the fact that Jesus died for it and that He is the savior of it (Eph. 5:23-25).

How many churches did God authorize? What were those whom the Lord added to the church called? "And the disciples were called Christians first in Antioch" (Acts 11:26). A true disciple of Christ will be called Christian, and will object to being called anything else. The Bible says nothing about different kinds of Christians, like Baptist Christian, Methodist Christian, or Presbyterian Christian. "Neither is there salvation in any other: for there is none other name under heaven given among men, whereby we must be saved" (Acts 4:12).

Yet again, the preacher has it wrong.

THE KINGDOM

Is it possible for God to make a mistake? By His own standard (Deuteronomy 18:22) God is a false prophet if not all of His prophesies come to pass. Is it strange to suggest that God could make a mistake? It shouldn't be. Preachers and other church leaders do it all the time. They say that God prophesied in the Old Testament that when Jesus would come to earth the first time (now 2000 years ago) He was going to establish a kingdom that would last forever. In fact, God did prophesy that. But today's preachers say that Jesus failed to do what God prophesied and that He established the church instead. They say His purpose was to establish a kingdom but He could not because of the rebellious Jews. If today's preachers are correct, Jesus also was mistaken when He preached, for He said the kingdom was "at hand" (Mark 1:15).

If Jesus failed to establish a kingdom when He came the first time, why should we think He'll be able to establish a kingdom when He comes back again? If He couldn't overcome the rebellious Jews in that small part of the world, how will He be able to overcome the six or seven billion people in the world today? Who knows how many people there will be when He does come back? Will He be able to persuade the Muslims, the Hindus and people of so many other religions in the world to support Him as King? No, if He couldn't deal with that small population of Jews, surely He'll not be able to deal with today's atheistic and heathen world!

The fact is, Jesus did establish a kingdom regardless of how often and how ardently the preacher stands up and denies it. Why do they deny it? Surely, some simply must just not know better. Others, perhaps, preach this false doctrine because of the sensation associated with

30

the idea that there will be a great war on earth following what they call a rapture, which, by the way, the Bible says nothing about. There is sensationalism associated with all the notions that modern day "prophets" teach regarding the end times. There are no "end times," plural; there is going to be just an "end time" as we shall see in a later chapter.

The misguided preachers get these ideas from the book of Revelation and the 24th chapter of Matthew. Jesus said in Matthew 24 that all those things prophesied there would take place before that generation passed away (verse 34). Those events prophesied in Matthew 24 did come to pass by the time Jerusalem was destroyed in AD 70. And the prophecies in the book of Revelation, John said twice, in the beginning of the book and at the end, were to shortly come to pass, and he said that they were symbolic ("signified," or put in signs or symbols) (Revelation 1:1 and 22:6).

Read the passages: "Verily I say unto you, This generation shall not pass, till all these things be fulfilled" Matt. 24:34). "The Revelation of Jesus Christ, which God gave unto him, to shew unto his servants things which must shortly come to pass; and he sent and signified *it* by his angel unto his servant John" (Rev. 1:1). "And he said unto me, These sayings *are* faithful and true: and the Lord God of the holy prophets sent his angel to shew unto his servants the things which must shortly be done" (Rev. 22:6). So this is not just a man disputing the words of today's preachers. It is Jesus Christ and the Apostle John disputing their words. Which would you rather believe? Wouldn't you rather believe Jesus and the Apostle John than today's preachers?

Now consider some of the passages that deal with both the prophesies in the Old Testament concerning the

31

coming of the kingdom and passages in the New Testament which show that the kingdom has already been established and that kingdom is the church and that Jesus is now King. These passages teach that not only is Jesus now King, but also that all true Christians today are subject to Him as King.

Before seeing the proof texts concerning the current existence of the kingdom there are three <u>very important</u> passages telling us about the nature of the kingdom. These should be kept in mind lest we make the same mistake the Jews of the first century made. You see, they were looking for a temporal kingdom, a physical kingdom with the Messiah sitting on a throne in Jerusalem. This is exactly what many preachers and church leaders of today believe and teach. They are making the same mistake made by the Jews who cried out for His crucifixion. Jesus said, "<u>My kingdom is not of this world</u>: if my kingdom were of this world, then would my servants fight" (John 18:36). "And when he was demanded of the Pharisees, when the kingdom of God should come, he answered them and said, <u>The kingdom of God cometh not with observation:</u> Neither shall they say, Lo here! or, lo there! for, behold, <u>the kingdom of God is within you</u>" (Luke 17:20-21). Now hear the words of the Apostle Paul: "For the kingdom of God is not meat and drink; but righteousness, and peace, and joy in the Holy Ghost" (Romans 14:17). The Kingdom of Christ is a spiritual kingdom. It never was and never will be a physical kingdom. (Emphasis is mine.)

Most all who call themselves Christian agree that the Old Testament did predict that Jesus was to come and set up a kingdom. Most, if not all, agree that this kingdom was to be set up during the days of the Roman Empire. The Old Testament Prophet Daniel, foretold this kingdom: "And in the days of these kings shall the God of heaven

32

set up a kingdom, which shall never be destroyed: and the kingdom shall not be left to other people, *but* it shall break in pieces and consume all these kingdoms, and it shall stand for ever" (Dan. 2:44). "The days of these kings" refer to the kings (or emperors) of Rome. So it was during the Roman Empire that Jesus set up His kingdom as predicted by Daniel.

Another important Old Testament passage is Daniel 7:13-14. Daniel saw in a vision Jesus ("one like the Son of man") going to God ("the Ancient of days") to receive dominion. (Dominion means power and authority.) When did Jesus go to God and receive dominion? In Matthew 28:18, Jesus said, "All power is given unto me in heaven and in earth." Mark tells us that after the Lord had said these words, "he was received up into heaven, and sat on the right hand of God" (Mark 16:19). So it was when Jesus went back into heaven that He received dominion.

Jesus is to continue to rule as King until the end, "Then *cometh* the end, when he shall have delivered up the kingdom to God, even the Father; when he shall have put down all rule and all authority and power. For he must reign, till he hath put all enemies under his feet. The last enemy *that* shall be destroyed *is* death" (1 Cor. 15:24-26). Jesus will reign over His subjects until the end of time, then He will give the kingdom to God the Father. Christians should be euphoric knowing they are in a kingdom ruled by Jesus and that eventually they, as a citizen of that kingdom, will be turned over to God our Creator. Paul said that Jesus will reign until the last enemy is destroyed, and the last enemy is death. Death will be destroyed when all men are resurrected.

Let's move to a few of the New Testament passages that teach the kingdom exists today. In the New Testament we learn that John the baptizer was the first to proclaim the eminent coming of the kingdom, saying, "Repent ye: for the kingdom of heaven is at hand" (Matt. 3:2). Then Jesus came teaching, and had His disciples teach, that the kingdom was "at hand." "From that time Jesus began to preach, and to say, Repent: for the kingdom of heaven is at hand" (Matt. 4:17). The instruction Jesus gave His disciples was, "as ye go, preach, saying, The kingdom of heaven is at hand" (Matt.10:7). This phrase "at hand" meant close by or right away or eminent. It is used many times in the Bible and always meant the same thing, close by or eminent.

Did Jesus not know what He was talking about? He said, "Verily I say unto you, That there be some of them that stand here, which shall not taste of death, till they have seen the kingdom of God come with power" (Mark 9:1) Unless the preacher wishes to argue with Jesus, how could he say that the kingdom has not come. Maybe he just believes there are some people living today who are 2000 years old. In light of Jesus' statement how could anyone argue that the kingdom is yet to be established?

We can identify the very day the kingdom started. Right before Jesus went back to heaven He instructed His disciples, "tarry ye in the city of Jerusalem, until ye be endued with power from on high" (Luke 24:49). As we just saw in Mark 9:1, the kingdom was to come with power. So if we can establish when the power came we will know when the kingdom came. "But ye shall receive power, after that the Holy Ghost is come upon you" (Acts 1:8). Now we need only to see when the Holy Ghost came on them to know when the power came. "And when the day of Pentecost was fully come" (Acts 2:1). "there appeared unto them cloven tongues like as of fire, and it sat upon each of them. And they were all filled with the Holy Ghost" (Acts 2:3-4). So the kingdom was started on this first Pentecost after the resurrection of Jesus. That's when the power came.

Keep in mind that Luke wrote the Gospel called Luke and he also wrote the book of Acts. He simply took up in Acts where he left off in Luke. This explains why you can leave Luke chapter 24 and go directly to Acts chapter one and have continuity of events that took place.

To confirm that the church and the kingdom are the same read carefully all of Hebrews 12:22-28. Here are quoted only excerpts: "But ye are come unto mount Sion, and unto the city of the living God, the heavenly Jerusalem, and to an innumerable company of angels, To the general assembly and church of the firstborn" (Heb.12:22-23). "Wherefore we receiving a kingdom which cannot be moved, let us have grace" (Heb. 12:28). Those Hebrew Christians had come to the church and had received the kingdom. Citizens in the kingdom constitute the church.

The kingdom was taught as "at hand" until after Jesus went back into heaven and until the day of Pentecost. From there forward the kingdom was spoken of as being in existence. Events of that Pentecost are recorded in Acts chapters one and two. On that day the Lord began adding converts to the church (Acts 2: 47). So we know that this is the beginning of the His church. Therefore, the Lord's church and the Lord's kingdom are the same and they were started on the first Pentecost following the resurrection of Jesus.

The preacher will tell you that Jesus had planned to establish a kingdom when He came the first time, but He failed and built the church instead.

We can see plainly that the kingdom exists today. Jesus is "King of kings" (Rev. 17:14). He couldn't be King without a kingdom. The Apostle Paul told the Colossian Christians that they were in the kingdom: Speaking of the Father "Who hath delivered us from the power of darkness, and hath translated *us* into the kingdom of his dear Son" (Col 1:13). What does it mean if it does not mean that Christians today are translated into the kingdom?

The apostle Paul charged the Thessalonian Christians to "walk worthy of God, who hath called you unto his kingdom and glory" (1 Thess. 2:12). If they were not called unto the Kingdom of Christ, unto what were they called? We don't know who wrote the Book of Hebrews, but it probably was Paul. Here it is made clear that we today can be in the Kingdom of Christ: "Wherefore we receiving a kingdom which cannot be moved, let us have grace, whereby we may serve God acceptably with reverence and godly fear" (Heb. 12:28). We can serve God acceptably only if we are in the Kingdom.

The Apostle John, as he began the Revelation of Jesus, in the last book of the Bible, claimed to be in the Kingdom already. "I John, who also am your brother, and companion in tribulation, and in the kingdom and patience of Jesus Christ, was in the isle that is called Patmos, for the word of God, and for the testimony of Jesus Christ" (Rev.1:9).

Does the Kingdom exist today? It takes a brave man to deny what Jesus and His apostles taught. But many do it today. Are they just misinformed? Are they just holding onto traditions that have evolved over the centuries? Are they not aware of these passages that teach the Kingdom is spiritual in nature and that it exists now with Jesus as King?

Jesus is King now and will reign as King until the end comes when He will deliver the kingdom up to God (I Cor. 15:24). "Then *cometh* the end, when he shall have delivered up the kingdom to God, even the Father; when he shall have put down all rule and all authority and power. For he must reign, till he hath put all enemies under his feet. The last enemy *that* shall be destroyed *is* death" (1 Cor. 15:24-26). Death will be destroyed when all of mankind are raised from death, the last enemy.

The preacher has it wrong!

ARE THE JEWS SPECIAL TODAY?

When Eve sinned in the Garden of Eden, God promised that in the seed of woman the head of the serpent, which had tempted her, would be bruised. God told the serpent, Satan, "I will put enmity between thee and the woman, and between thy seed and her seed; it shall bruise thy head, and thou shalt bruise his heel" (Gen. 3:15). The Bible, from that point, is God's revelation of the fulfilling of that promise.

After the flood, when the world was going into idolatry again, God choose Abram (whose name meant exalted father) to be the one through whom the promised seed should come. Abram was living in the land of Ur, in Mesopotamia, modern-day Iraq. Abram's name was later changed to Abraham, the meaning of which was father of many nations.

Abraham was a righteous man, a believer in God. We read later in the Book of Genesis that his faith in God was so strong that he was willing to sacrifice his son for God. This had to be an awful trial of his faith. Abraham was the granddaddy of all Jews.

The whole purpose of the Jewish nation was to prepare a people for the coming of the Messiah, Jesus Christ, the seed of woman, who was to come to bruise Satan's head.

Not enough emphasis can be placed on the fact that the whole purpose of the Jewish nation was to prepare for the coming of the Lord. When this purpose was fulfilled there was no longer any need for a distinct people who would not forget God as most of the world apparently had done. If the preacher understood this he might not be confusing his congregation with his wild notions and spectacular ideas about the so-called "end times."

"Now the Lord had said unto Abram, Get thee out of thy country, and from thy kindred, and from thy father's house, unto a land that I will shew thee: And I will make of thee a great nation, and I will bless thee, and make thy name great; and thou shalt be a blessing: And I will bless them that bless thee, and curse him that curseth thee: and in thee shall all families of the earth be blessed" (Gen. 12:1-3). God had Abram to go into the land of Canaan, and there "the Lord appeared unto Abram, and said, Unto thy seed will I give this land" (Gen. 12:7). By the time we get to Genesis chapter fifteen, the promise seems to have taken on the form of a covenant, for it says the Lord made a covenant with Abram saying, "Unto thy seed have I given this land, from the river of Egypt unto the great river, the river Euphrates" (Gen. 15:18). This is significant because it tells us the extent of the land promised to Abraham.

There are two aspects to the promise God made to Abraham. One aspect was material in nature the other was spiritual. The first aspect involved his descendents becoming a "great nation" and their receiving the land. The spiritual aspect was that through him "all families of the earth be blessed." So if we can find in the Bible when Abraham's descendents became a great nation and when they received the land we will know that the material aspect of the promise was fulfilled (and, therefore, not something we look forward to in our future). Of course, we know that with the coming of Christ the spiritual aspect of the promise was fulfilled.

Abraham had two sons, Isaac and Ishmael. Isaac was the one chosen to receive the same promise Abraham had received. Isaac's son was Jacob. Jacob had twelve sons. Joseph, Jacob's next to the youngest son, seemed to be his father's favorite. The older brothers were jealous so they wanted to dispose of Joseph. Joseph was sold to

39

traders who sold him again in Egypt where he ended up as a slave. Joseph gained favor, though, in the eyes of Pharaoh and received a position of high authority in Egypt.

Because of a famine back in Canaan, Jacob's home-land, Jacob's whole family ended up moving to Egypt where they grew into a great nation composed of twelve tribes.

The Jews (Hebrews) were so numerous by the time of Moses' birth that Pharaoh decided to have all male children thrown into the River Nile. Moses' mother hid him, and Pharaohs daughter found him and raised him as her own. Moses grew up and led the children of Israel out of Egypt and to the promised land. Genesis 15:14 says they shall "come out with great substance." So they were going to take much wealth with them from Egypt.

By this point the Hebrews had grown into a great nation. Surely they would be a greater nation before the coming of King Solomon who, as we shall see, ruled over all the land promised to Abraham.

All the priests among the Jews came from the tribe of Levi. Since the Levites were to be scattered over the whole promised land, the sons of Joseph (Ephraim and Manasseh) each was to be the father of a tribe. Besides Joseph and Levi, the other ten sons of Jacob were the heads of different tribes making a total of twelve.

By the time the Jews got into Canaan Joshua was their leader. Moses, at some point, had disobeyed God so he was not allowed to enter Canaan. Regarding the land, there is an important passage written by Joshua, found in Joshua 21:43-45: "And the Lord gave unto Israel all the land which he sware to give unto their fathers; and they possessed it, and dwelt therein." "There failed not ought of any good thing which the Lord had spoken unto the house of Israel; all came to pass" (Joshua 21:43 and 45).

By the time of Solomon, "Judah and Israel *were* many, as the sand which *is* by the sea in multitude, eating and drinking, and making merry. And Solomon reigned over all kingdoms from the river unto the land of the Philistines, and unto the border of Egypt: they brought presents, and served Solomon all the days of his life" (1 Kings 4:20-21). King Solomon reigned over all the land God had promised.

Now we see that the children of Israel became a great nation and that they had received the land that God had promised to give them. "There failed not ought" of anything that God had promised concerning the land and their "nation" status; "all came to pass." The material aspect of the promise was fulfilled.

Let's go back and trace the promise from Abraham to Moses, some four hundred years later. Watch for the promise to be renewed to Abraham's son, Isaac, then to Isaac's son, Jacob, whose name was changed to Israel. Jacob had twelve sons. Did they all receive all of the promise made to Abraham?

In Genesis 26:1-4, we learn that the Lord told Isaac to go to Egypt and "dwell in the land which I shall tell thee of: Sojourn in this land, and I will be with thee, and will bless thee; for unto thee, and unto thy seed, I will give all these countries, and I will perform the oath which I sware unto Abraham thy father; And I will make thy seed to multiply as the stars of heaven, and will give unto thy seed all these countries; and in thy seed shall all the nations of the earth be blessed." So, Isaac received the same promise that his father, Abraham, had received,

41

with both the spiritual and the material aspects. Of course, this was some time before the family went into Egypt.

Isaac's son, Jacob, was on his way to get a wife when he had a dream. In his dream he saw a ladder from earth to heaven. "And, behold, the Lord stood above it, and said, I *am* the Lord God of Abraham thy father, and the God of Isaac: the land whereon thou liest, to thee will I give it, and to thy seed; And thy seed shall be as the dust of the earth, and thou shalt spread abroad to the west, and to the east, and to the north, and to the south: and in thee and in thy seed shall all the families of the earth be blessed" (Gen. 28:13-14). So, now Jacob received the same promise.

Where do we go from here? Jacob had twelve sons. Which one would receive the promise? We have to move on through the book of Genesis to see. In the forty-ninth chapter we learn that Jacob's son, Judah, was the one through whom all the nations of the earth were to be blessed. "The sceptre shall not depart from Judah, nor a lawgiver from between his feet, until Shiloh come; and unto him *shall* the gathering of the people *be*" (Gen. 49:10). All nations of the earth would receive the blessing of Shiloh the Prince of peace. King David was of the tribe of Judah. Jesus descended from David and inherited the throne. So Judah was head of the tribe through which Jesus came, the tribe through which all nations of the earth would be blessed. But what about the "nation" and "land" aspect of the promise?

As God was preparing Moses to deliver the children of Israel from Egyptian bondage, He told Moses to tell the people, "I *am* the Lord your God, which bringeth you out from under the burdens of the Egyptians. And I will bring you in unto the land, concerning the which I did swear to

42

give it to Abraham, to Isaac, and to Jacob; and I will give it you for an heritage: I *am* the Lord" (Ex. 6:1-8). So, all the Israelites received the promise that they would receive the land that had been promised to Abraham. Only Judah received the spiritual part of the promise.

We have seen that God made a promise and kept it regarding the Jews becoming a nation and receiving the Land of Canaan. But there's more. They had received the land, but would they keep it?

Before the Israelites entered into the promised land, God made another covenant with them. This covenant was made at Moab after the Jews had wandered in the wilderness for forty years. We read about this covenant in Deuteronomy chapters twenty-eight through thirty. This covenant is often referred to as the "covenant of blessing and curse." If the Jews were faithful to God they would prosper. If they were unfaithful they would be cursed. One of the curses about which we read in chapter 28, verses 21 and 63, is that if they were unfaithful they would be removed from the promised land. They were told in chapter 30, that if they repented they would return.

The promise to Abraham was unconditional. They were going to receive the land no matter what. But the covenant (or promises) made at Moab was conditional; the Jews had to remain faithful to keep the land.

Read the threats: "The Lord shall make the pestilence cleave unto thee, until he have consumed thee from off the land, whither thou goest to possess it" (Deut. 28:21). "And it shall come to pass, *that* as the Lord rejoiced over you to do you good, and to multiply you; so the Lord will rejoice over you to destroy you, and to bring you to nought; and ye shall be plucked from off the land whither

43

thou goest to possess it" (Deut. 28:63). "I denounce unto you this day, that ye shall surely perish, *and that* ye shall not prolong *your* days upon the land, whither thou passest over Jordan to go to possess it" (Deut. 30:18).

As we read on through their history, we learn that the Jews did become unfaithful. After King Solomon died the kingdom was divided. Jereboam ruled Israel in the north, and Reheboam ruled Judah in the south. Israel was taken into Assyrian captivity. It is generally believed that they were removed from the land about 721 BC. Judah was taken into Babylonian captivity. They are thought to have been removed from the land about 586 BC.

God had told them back at Moab that if they repented of their sins after being taken away, they would be able to return. Isaiah prophesied that only a remnant would return. "The remnant shall return, *even* the remnant of Jacob, unto the mighty God. For though thy people Israel be as the sand of the sea, *yet* a remnant of them shall return" (Isaiah 10:21-22).

Jeremiah, the prophet, also predicted the return of a remnant to Israel. "And I will gather the remnant of my flock out of all countries whither I have driven them, and will bring them again to their folds; and they shall be fruitful and increase" (Jer. 23:3).

After the remnant returned, the scriptures speak of their return in the past tense. The Old Testament writers, after the remnant came home, spoke as though the remnant had already come home. Haggai 1:12-14, for example, speaks of the remnant rebuilding the temple of the Lord. (The Joshua in this chapter, of course, is a different Joshua from the one mentioned earlier.) "all the remnant of the people, obeyed the voice of the Lord" (Hag. 1:12). Zechariah 8:6, 11-12, also mention the remnant who were rebuilding in the city of Jerusalem after their return from captivity. These are just two instances showing the remnant had returned. But two are enough. The remnant had returned.

God kept His promise to Abraham. He also kept His promises made at Moab regarding the Jews. The only thing left for the Jews was the promise that through Abraham and his seed all nations of the earth would be blessed. The earth was blessed with the coming of Christ, whose earthly parents descended from Abraham. This was the fulfillment of the promise to Satan in the garden of Eden, as well as the fulfillment of the promise to Abraham.

Since all the promises made to the Jews have been fulfilled, there is nothing more for them except what they can receive through Christ, along with the rest of us.

"For ye are all the children of God by faith in Christ Jesus. For as many of you as have been baptized into Christ have put on Christ. There is neither Jew nor Greek, there is neither bond nor free, there is neither male nor female: for ye are all one in Christ Jesus. And if ye *be* Christ's, then are ye Abraham's seed, and heirs according to the promise" (Gal. 3:26-29). There is neither Jew nor Greek! Christians today constitute spiritual Israel, Abraham's seed. Read Gal 3:7: "Know ye therefore that they which are of faith, the same are the children of Abraham." This includes Jews and Gentiles alike.

It's amazing that so many people today believe the Jews now are different somehow in the eyes of God. They served the purpose for which God set them aside. They were simply a people chosen to be the ones through whom Jesus would come.

45

The preacher has it wrong!

CALVINISM -- Part One

John Calvin was raised a Catholic. He was born in France on July 10, 1509, and died May 27, 1564. He is responsible for a system of theology followed by many people today. Calvin was a preacher who may have done more harm than any other protestant leader since people began leaving the Catholic church.

An acronym is used to identify Calvin's various theories. The acronym is TULIP. Many preachers, teachers and whole churches hold to all or some of Calvin's doctrines. The "T" is for "Total Depravity." This is a theory that says babies are born depraved. The idea is that we inherit Adam's sin. The "U" is for "Unconditional Election." The idea here is that God determined before the world began who would be saved and who would be lost, and nothing can be done to change this. The "L" stands for "Limited Atonement." Under this theory, Jesus died for only some but not for all people. The "I" represents "Irresistible Grace." This means that God sends the Holy Spirit, and He sends Him to only those He predestined to be saved. He sends the Holy Spirit in order for those people to have their depraved nature removed so that they can believe and understand the scriptures. And, by the way, these people cannot do anything to stop the Holy Spirit from doing this to them. The "P" is for "Perseverance of the Saints." This means once saved, always saved. There is nothing you can do bad enough to keep you out of heaven once you are saved.

We don't need the Bible to tell us but once for us to accept what is being said. For example, if the Bible tells us once to jump off a cliff, we don't need to be told in several more scriptures to jump off a cliff. Once is enough. The point is, if we are told once that we are not born depraved, then we don't need to be told again. But

47

the fact is we are told in several places that we don't inherit Adam's sin. The preacher says that we are born depraved, and that we do inherit Adam's sin. If one scripture tells us that we are not born in sin, the preacher is wrong. But there are many places in the scriptures where we learn that we are not born in sin. This principle applies to the other false doctrines of Calvin.

At this point let's suppose that most churches, the preachers and church leaders, hold to Calvin's doctrines. Should it be surprising? Jesus said, "Enter ye in at the strait gate: for wide *is* the gate, and broad *is* the way, that leadeth to destruction, and many there be which go in threat: Because strait *is* the gate, and narrow *is* the way, which leadeth unto life, and few there be that find it" (Matt. 7:13-14). It would take a proud and vain man to say he has all the answers. No one does. But anyone can look at the scriptures to see what they say! According to Jesus, it looks like most people will be lost. Consider how many Jews cried out "crucify," and how many were sympathetic to the Lord at His death. Not many were sympathetic. Only eight souls were saved in the days of Noah. Don't be surprised that many, many people are mistaken and that the preacher is wrong.

Are babies born depraved, those vile little rascals? Whatever passages the misguided preacher is using to make his point, he must be misunderstanding, or maybe he is misunderstanding the context from which he's taking the passages.

Could the preacher be using Psalms 51:5, to make his point? "Behold, I was shapen in iniquity; and in sin did my mother conceive me." Here David is not speaking of himself. He's speaking as though he were the baby that died having been born as a result of David's sin with another man's wife. It says <u>his mother</u> sinned conceiving him. Of course David sinned also.

Where in the Bible does it say that babies are born in sin? <u>Nowhere!</u> Where in the Bible does it say anything about babies inheriting Adam's sin? <u>Nowhere!</u> Isaiah said, "But your iniquities have separated between you and your God, and your sins have hid *his* face from you, that he will not hear" (Isaiah 59:2). For us to become separated from God we have to first be with Him. Babies are with Him at first, then when they begin to sin they part company with God.

"The soul that sinneth, it shall die. The son shall not bear the iniquity of the father, neither shall the father bear the iniquity of the son: the righteousness of the righteous shall be upon him, and the wickedness of the wicked shall be upon him" (Ezek. 18:20). Did you know that some churches teach that if a baby is not baptized it will go to hell?

The prophet Ezekiel said, "The word of the Lord came unto me again, saying, What mean ye, that ye use this proverb concerning the land of Israel, saying, The fathers have eaten sour grapes, and the children's teeth are set on edge? *As* I live, saith the Lord God, ye shall not have *occasion* any more to use this proverb in Israel. Behold, all souls are mine; as the soul of the father, so also the soul of the son is mine: the soul that sinneth, it shall die" (Ezek. 18:1-4). It looks like he is telling them to never say again that a child is responsible for his father's sins. In other words, children don't inherit their father's sins.

God told Ezekiel, the prophet, to say to the king of Tyrus, "Thou *wast* perfect in thy ways from the day that thou wast created, till iniquity was found in thee" (Ezek. 28:12-15). Not until iniquity was found in the king of Tyrus,

49

was he no longer perfect in his behavior. If he didn't repent he would die.

One more Old Testament passage indicating that we go astray after birth: "Lo, this only have I found, that God hath made man upright; but they have sought out many inventions" (Eccl. 7:29). Obviously Solomon here is referring to sins that man had invented. If he were talking about making Adam upright he would not have said "they," indicating more people than just the one man Adam that God had created upright. All people are created (or born) upright.

If babies were sinners at birth Jesus didn't know it or He would never have said, "Verily I say unto you, Except ye be converted, and become as little children, ye shall not enter into the kingdom of heaven" (Matt. 18:3). On another occasion He said, "Suffer little children, and forbid them not, to come unto me: for of such is the kingdom of heaven" (Matt. 19:13-14). So people like babies constitute the Kingdom of heaven. These two passages are perhaps the most certain proof that we are not born in sin.

"Behold, the Lord's hand is not shortened, that it cannot save; neither his ear heavy, that it cannot hear: But your iniquities have separated between you and your God, and your sins have hid *his* face from you, that he will not hear" (Isaiah 59:1-2). Babies don't sin. Babies can't sin!

Sin is not something we inherit. Instead, sin is something we do. "Whosoever committeth sin transgresseth also the law: for sin is the transgression of the law" (1 John 3:4). Your sister can give you her sins as easily as your father can give you his.

"But I say unto you, That every idle word that men shall speak, they shall give account thereof in the day of judgment. For by thy words thou shalt be justified, and by thy words thou shalt be condemned" (Matt. 12:36-37). We are justified or condemned by what we say or do, not by what Adam did. Romans 2:5-6 tells us that God "will render to every man according to his deeds."

The Apostle Paul said we will appear before Christ that "every one may receive the things *done* in *his* body, according to that he hath done, whether *it be* good or bad" (2 Cor. 5:10). This doesn't say that we will appear before Him to be judged by what Adam did. Peter didn't believe we inherit Adam's sins. He said God will judge "according to every man's work, pass the time of your sojourning *here* in fear" (1 Peter 1:17).

Did it ever occur to the preacher that if Calvin is wrong regarding inheriting sin, he may be wrong about other things he taught? Even in the Old Testament the prophets didn't believe that babies inherited Adams sins. Isaiah said, "your iniquities have separated between you and your God, and your sins have hid *his* face from you, that he will not hear" (Isaiah 59:2).

The preacher is wrong.

Having dealt with the doctrine of Total Hereditary Depravity (babies inherit their parent's sins), let's now look at the passages that people mistakenly believe teach some of the other doctrines of Calvin: Unconditional Election, Limited Atonement, and Irresistible Grace. Calvin's doctrine of Perseverance of the Saints, or "once saved, always saved," will be dealt with later.

On the surface, it may look like the Bible is teaching that God predetermined before the world began specifically which individuals will be saved. It's not necessary to say that God doesn't make mistakes, that He is not the author of confusion or that the Bible does not contradict itself. If anyone believes any of these things is true, he has a problem and needs to start his Bible study all over again. We must believe the Bible is totally dependable and reliable. But what about those scriptures that the preacher believes teach Calvin's doctrines?

"Blessed *be* the God and Father of our Lord Jesus Christ, who hath blessed us with all spiritual blessings in heavenly *places* in Christ: According as he hath chosen us in him before the foundation of the world, that we should be holy and without blame before him in love: Having predestinated us unto the adoption of children by Jesus Christ to himself, according to the good pleasure of his will" (Eph. 1:3-5).

"And we know that all things work together for good to them that love God, to them who are the called according to *his* purpose. For whom he did foreknow, he also did predestinate *to be* conformed to the image of his Son, that he might be the firstborn among many brethren. Moreover whom he did predestinate, them he also called:

and whom he called, them he also justified: and whom he justified, them he also glorified" (Romans 8:28-30).

The Bible definitely teaches predestination, but not of the sort the preacher teaches today. Plainly stated, <u>God determined before the world began that those who conform to His will would be saved</u>. If this is not what it means these passages contradict many other passages in the Bible. Does God contradict Himself? If these scriptures are referring to specific individuals what do you do with the following scriptures?

First, the Apostle, Paul made it plain that God had a plan: "But we speak the wisdom of God in a mystery, *even* the hidden *wisdom,* which God ordained before the world unto our glory" (1 Cor. 2:7). This plan was for the redemption of and justification for those who love Him. It was called a mystery because it had been hidden or unknown by man until salvation came by the death and resurrection of Christ. God planned the Christian system before the world began. He determined what sort of people we should be.

The following passages should be sufficient to show that Calvin and his followers are wrong when teaching their false theories of Unconditional Election (predestination), Limited Atonement (Christ died for only some people), and Irresistible Grace (God is going to save certain people whether they like it or not). All three of these theories fall together.

In Acts 10:34-35, after the first Gentiles were converted, "Then Peter opened *his* mouth, and said, Of a truth I perceive that God is no respecter of persons: But in every nation he that feareth him, and worketh righteousness, is accepted with him." The next verse says, "he is Lord of all." We could stop here; this is enough to show that God

53

had not chosen, before the world began, only specific individuals to be saved.

The Apostle, Paul made an even more emphatic statement when writing to Titus: "For the grace of God that bringeth salvation hath appeared to all men" (Titus 2:11). All men have access to salvation. Writing to the Corinthians, he said, "But glory, honour, and peace, to every man that worketh good, to the Jew first, and also to the Gentile: For there is no respect of persons with God" (Romans 2:10-11). The promise is to "every man" who works good.

Why would Jesus have instructed His disciples to "Go ye into all the world, and preach the gospel to every creature. He that believeth and is baptized shall be saved; but he that believeth not shall be damned" (Mark 16:15-16)? He didn't say those whom God had chosen would be saved, but He said, "he that believeth." Many people have believed and have waited for the Holy Spirit to come upon them, and in distress have given up, thinking that they must be among the ones God had not chosen. That's a bad place to be. How, if Calvin was right, could they have believed in the first place? It sounds like Calvin, in this case, is responsible for those people giving up and finally being lost. It's a cruel and vile doctrine.

In case you are thinking that he who believes, having been taught, can believe only after the Holy Spirit changes his heart. You are right, but not in the sense that Calvin taught. The Holy Spirit does change our hearts when we are exposed to the Word that He left the apostles, and those words are written down now in the Bible. Before Jesus went back into heaven He promised to send a Comforter which is the Holy Spirit. This Comforter would remind the apostles of the things Jesus had taught them and teach them "all things." "But the Comforter, *which is* the Holy Ghost, whom the Father will

54

send in my name, he shall teach you all things, and bring all things to your remembrance, whatsoever I have said unto you" (John 14:26). The Holy Ghost came on the day of Pentecost (Acts 2). From there He began delivering the Word to the apostles. These words, the gospel, we now have written in the Bible. It's the Bible that moves us; it motivates us to obey. "For I am not ashamed of the gospel of Christ: for it is the power of God unto salvation to every one that believeth" (Romans 1:16). There is power in the Word. Our conviction comes not by some miraculous experience.

If that doesn't convince you, look at Heb. 2:9: "But we see Jesus, who was made a little lower than the angels for the suffering of death, crowned with glory and honour; that he by the grace of God should taste death for every man". This passage specifically addresses the question of "limited atonement," the question as to whether or not Jesus died for all men. Actually, it proves Calvin wrong also on predestination and irresistible grace. So do the following passages; they speak for themselves.

Of Jesus, the Apostle, John said, "he is the propitiation for our sins: and not for ours only, but also for *the sins of* the whole world" (1 John 2:1-2).

John the baptizer told his audience regarding Jesus, "Behold the Lamb of God, which taketh away the sin of the world" (John 1:29). Jesus died in order to save any one in the world who would obey him, not just certain ones whom God had chosen before the world began.

"And if ye call on the Father, who without respect of persons judgeth according to every man's work, pass the time of your sojourning *here* in fear" (1 Peter 1:17). We will be judged by what we do. God is not a respecter of persons.

"The Lord is not slack concerning his promise, as some men count slackness; but is longsuffering to us-ward, not willing that any should perish, but that all should come to repentance" (2 Peter 3:9). How could the preacher possibly argue with this? Jesus died for everyone. How could anyone attend this preacher's church?

"For this *is* good and acceptable in the sight of God our Saviour; Who will have all men to be saved, and to come unto the knowledge of the truth" (1 Tim. 2:3-4). It's God's will that <u>all men</u> be saved. The preacher argues that no one can come to the knowledge of the truth until the Holy Spirit acts on him somehow. Paul said that God's will is to have all men "come unto the knowledge of the truth." The preacher argues that no one has the capacity to come to the knowledge of the truth until the Holy Spirit does His work. The Holy Spirit did His work regarding the truth when He delivered the Word to the apostles. Read John chapter seventeen.

The next two passages tell us that we are responsible for our own salvation: "And with many other words did he testify and exhort, saying, Save yourselves from this untoward generation" (Acts 2:40), and "Wherefore, my beloved, as ye have always obeyed, not as in my presence only, but now much more in my absence, work out your own salvation with fear and trembling" (Phil. 2:12).

We will be judged according to what we do. "For we must all appear before the judgment seat of Christ; that every one may receive the things *done* in *his* body, according to that he hath done, whether *it be* good or bad" (2 Cor. 5:10).

Peter warns, in I Peter 5:8, "Be sober, be vigilant; because your adversary the devil, as a roaring lion, walketh about, seeking whom he may devour." The devil wouldn't waste

56

his time trying to lead man astray knowing God is going to save all whom He had specifically chosen.

These passages prove beyond any doubt that Calvin and all who follow his teachings are wrong, specifically regarding those doctrines of Unconditional Election, Limited Atonement, and Irresistible Grace.

All this makes our efforts even more urgent. And it makes understanding and obeying the gospel more important. "For I am not ashamed of the gospel of Christ: for it is the power of God unto salvation to every one that believeth; to the Jew first, and also to the Greek" (Romans 1:16). Every man can accept and obey the gospel and be saved.

So, do we have a contradiction in the scriptures? Or does the preacher just have it wrong? God predestinated that all who conform to His will shall be saved. And He made this determination before the world began.

The preacher has it wrong.

If you believe that a Christian cannot be lost after being saved, the following scriptures and the thoughts that accompany them should change your mind.

If the doctrine called Perseverance of the Saints (once saved always saved) is true, one who is not a Christian can tell a simple lie, and never sin again, and be lost in hell forever. And a Christian who rapes and murders will be saved even if he never repents. This questions God's justice. It questions God's moral character. It questions God's intelligence! The very idea that one could teach these doctrines in light of all the scriptures is utter nonsense.

In order to know what God's attitude has always been, let's look first at some Old Testament passages. Let's start with Ezekiel.

"Again, when a righteous *man* doth turn from his righteousness, and commit iniquity, and I lay a stumblingblock before him, he shall die: because thou hast not given him warning, he shall die in his sin, and his righteousness which he hath done shall not be remembered; but his blood will I require at thine hand. Nevertheless if thou warn the righteous *man*, that the righteous sin not, and he doth not sin, he shall surely live, because he is warned; also thou hast delivered thy soul" (Ezek. 3:20-21). This also suggests that if we do not warn the righteous man who sins our souls are also at risk.

Further, Ezekiel said, "But when the righteous turneth away from his righteousness, and committeth iniquity, *and* doeth according to all the abominations that the wicked *man* doeth, shall he live? All his righteousness

58

that he hath done shall not be mentioned: in his trespass that he hath trespassed, and in his sin that he hath sinned, in them shall he die" (Ezek. 18:24).

"When a righteous *man* turneth away from his righteousness, and committeth iniquity, and dieth in them; for his iniquity that he hath done shall he die. Again, when the wicked *man* turneth away from his wickedness that he hath committed, and doeth that which is lawful and right, he shall save his soul alive" (Ezek. 18:26-27). When Ezekiel speaks of the righteous man turning bad and dying, we know that he was talking about him losing his soul, because verse 27 says that a bad man who repents will save his soul. Are you aware that some preachers teach that a righteous man is not capable of sinning?

The preacher who believes and teaches that a Christian can't sin gets the idea from I John 3:9. John did say one born of God cannot sin. "Whosoever is born of God doth not commit sin; for his seed remaineth in him: and he cannot sin, because he is born of God." If this means what the preacher says it does, why did John say, "If we say that we have no sin, we deceive ourselves, and the truth is not in us" (1 John 1:8)? And why did he say, "My little children, these things write I unto you, that ye sin not" (I John 2:1)? And if a Christian is not capable of sinning, why did John say, "if any man sin, we have an advocate with the Father" (1 John 2:1)? Study the words and the grammar of the original language, and you learn that John was saying whosoever is born of God does not keep on committing sin; for his seed remains in him, and he cannot keep on sinning.

Jesus just wasted His time when He gave the parable of the sower, for He said the seed that fell "on the rock *are they*, which, when they hear, receive the word with joy;

59

and these have no root, which for a while believe, and in time of temptation fall away" (Luke 8:13). These are people who were converted and fell away. Jesus also said, "No man, having put his hand to the plough, and looking back, is fit for the kingdom of God" (Luke 9:62). How could one who is not fit for the kingdom of God be saved? Jesus is referring to saved people, believing people who fall away.

Jesus said further, "I am the true vine, and my Father is the husbandman. Every branch in me that beareth not fruit he taketh away. . . . As the branch cannot bear fruit of itself, except it abide in the vine; no more can ye, except ye abide in me. . . . If a man abide not in me, he is cast forth as a branch, and is withered; and men gather them, and cast *them* into the fire, and they are burned" (John 15:1-6). The phrase, "except it abide in the vine," tells us that it is possible to not abide in the vine. He who does not abide in the vine is cast into the fire and burned. These are words of the Savior Himself. This is Jesus saying Calvin and the preacher are wrong. If this doesn't mean that a Christian can fall and be lost, what does it mean?

The Apostle Paul, passing by Ephesus, called for the elders of the church to come to him, and he warned them, "Take heed therefore unto yourselves, and to all the flock, over the which the Holy Ghost hath made you overseers, to feed the church of God, which he hath purchased with his own blood. For I know this, that after my departing shall grievous wolves enter in among you, not sparing the flock. Also of your own selves shall men arise, speaking perverse things, to draw away disciples after them" (Acts 20:28-30).

The Apostle Paul was not concerned just about others; he was also concerned about himself. "I therefore so run, not

60

as uncertainly; so fight I, not as one that beateth the air: But I keep under my body, and bring *it* into subjection: lest that by any means, when I have preached to others, I myself should be a castaway" (1 Cor. 9:26-27).

The Old Testament was written so we could learn from the examples found there. "Now all these things happened unto them for ensamples: and they are written for our admonition, upon whom the ends of the world are come. Wherefore let him that thinketh he standeth take heed lest he fall" (1 Cor. 10:11-12). Many people in the Old Testament fell from Gods grace. Paul, in writing to Christians, warned them to be certain they not likewise fall while thinking they were on good terms with God.

Apparently some Christians at Galatia were trying to practice part of the Old Testament Law and be faithful to Christ at the same time. Paul points out that circumcision isn't required anymore, and if they try to be justified by the old law they "are fallen from grace." Why would he say this if one could not fall from grace. Grace is God's unmerited favor. If they fall from grace, they lose God's favor. Paul said, "For I testify again to every man that is circumcised, that he is a debtor to do the whole law. Christ is become of no effect unto you, whosoever of you are justified by the law; ye are fallen from grace" (Gal. 5:3-4). How could Christians lose God's favor and hope to be saved? Keep in mind that Paul was writing to Christians (chapter one, verse two). He had already told them, "I marvel that ye are so soon removed from him that called you into the grace of Christ unto another gospel" (Gal. 1:6).

Whether or not we are Christians, it seems reasonable that we should "Be not deceived; God is not mocked: for whatsoever a man soweth, that shall he also reap" (Gal. 6:7). A saved person who decides to continually sin will reap the results. "For the wages of sin *is* death; but the gift of God *is* eternal life through Jesus Christ our Lord" (Romans 6:23). We see here that death is the opposite of eternal life. So death means being lost eternally.

"This charge I commit unto thee, son Timothy, according to the prophecies which went before on thee, that thou by them mightest war a good warfare; Holding faith, and a good conscience; which some having put away concerning faith have made shipwreck: Of whom is Hymenaeus and Alexander; whom I have delivered unto Satan, that they may learn not to blaspheme" (1 Tim. 1:18-20). These two brothers were delivered to Satan because they had "made shipwreck" of the faith.

"Now the Spirit speaketh expressly, that in the latter times some shall depart from the faith, giving heed to seducing spirits, and doctrines of devils" (1 Tim. 4:1).

"But if any provide not for his own, and specially for those of his own house, he hath denied the faith, and is worse than an infidel" (1 Tim. 5:8).

"But they that will be rich fall into temptation and a snare, and *into* many foolish and hurtful lusts, which drown men in destruction and perdition. For the love of money is the root of all evil: which while some coveted after, they have erred from the faith, and pierced themselves through with many sorrows" (1 Tim. 6:9-10).

"But shun profane *and* vain babblings: for they will increase unto more ungodliness. And their word will eat as doth a canker: of whom is Hymenaeus and Philetus; Who concerning the truth have erred, saying that the resurrection is past already; and overthrow the faith of some" (2 Tim. 2:16-18).

What a dreadful thought to imagine being separated from God throughout eternity. But it must be possible for a saved person to lose his salvation. Notice the warning to Hebrew Christians: "Take heed, brethren, lest there be in any of you an evil heart of unbelief, in departing from the living God" (Heb. 3:12). You cannot depart from God unless you are saved first. He's writing to brethren, therefore, to Christians who were at risk of departing from God.

"Let us therefore fear, lest, a promise being left *us* of entering into his rest, any of you should seem to come short of it" (Heb. 4:1). "Come short of it?" "Come short of it?" Why fear if once we are saved we are always saved? It couldn't be any more plain. The writer is warning Christians against falling and being lost.

"Let us labour therefore to enter into that rest, lest any man fall after the same example of unbelief" (Heb. 4:11). Can man fall? This passage says so.

"For *it is* impossible for those who were once enlightened, and have tasted of the heavenly gift, and were made partakers of the Holy Ghost, . . .If they shall fall away, to renew them again unto repentance; seeing they crucify to themselves the Son of God afresh, and put *him* to an open shame" (Heb. 6:4-8). He goes on to compare them to briers which are to be burned.

Speaking of those who had been "sanctified" (Heb. 10:29), if they sin "willfully," "there remains no more sacrifice for sins, But a certain fearful looking for of judgment and fiery indignation." He then, in chapter 10, compares those who violate Moses' law to those who violate Christ's law. Those who violate Moses' law died without mercy. The writer asks, "Of how much sorer punishment, suppose ye, shall he be thought worthy, who hath

63

trodden under foot the Son of God, and hath counted the blood of the covenant, wherewith he was sanctified, an unholy thing?" (Heb. 10:29) Then he says in verse 30, "The Lord shall judge his people." He goes on to admonish, "Cast not away therefore your confidence, which hath great recompence of reward. For ye have need of patience, that, after ye have done the will of God, ye might receive the promise" (Heb. 10:26-36). Because they were said to be sanctified we know that they were Christians. He's encouraging Christians to be sure they receive the promise.

Why would the Lord judge His people if the preacher is right and the Lord's people cannot be lost? Why not just take that list God made of the saved before time began and take them on to heaven instead of bothering to judge them?

"Now the just shall live by faith: but if *any man* draw back, my soul shall have no pleasure in him. But we are not of them who draw back unto perdition; but of them that believe to the saving of the soul" (Heb. 10:38-39). "No pleasure." Some believe to the saving of the soul, then there are those who do not. Again, the book of Hebrews was to and about Christians.

"Brethren, if any of you do err from the truth, and one convert him; Let him know, that he which converteth the sinner from the error of his way shall save a soul from death, and shall hide a multitude of sins" (James 5:19-20). We can be certain that James is talking about Christians because he called those whom he addressed as "brethren." If a brother falls and another convert him, he saves his soul.

Peter warned Christians to "Be sober, be vigilant; because your adversary the devil, as a roaring lion, walketh about,

64

seeking whom he may devour" (1 Peter 5:8). Can the devil devour one once he is saved? Christians were the ones Peter was addressing. So, yes, the devil can devour a wayward Christian.

Peter's comments in 2 Peter 2:20-22 need no explanation: "For if after they have escaped the pollutions of the world through the knowledge of the Lord and Saviour Jesus Christ, they are again entangled therein, and overcome, the latter end is worse with them than the beginning. For it had been better for them not to have known the way of righteousness, than, after they have known *it*, to turn from the holy commandment delivered unto them. But it is happened unto them according to the true proverb, The dog *is* turned to his own vomit again; and the sow that was washed to her wallowing in the mire." How could his latter end be worse than the first unless his soul is lost?

"Ye therefore, beloved, seeing ye know *these things* before, beware lest ye also, being led away with the error of the wicked, fall from your own stedfastness" (2 Peter 3:17). The preacher says you cannot fall. The holy Apostle Peter says you can. Whom will you believe?

Writing to a Christian, The Apostle John said, "Look to yourselves, that we lose not those things which we have wrought, but that we receive a full reward. Whosoever transgresseth, and abideth not in the doctrine of Christ, hath not God. He that abideth in the doctrine of Christ, he hath both the Father and the Son" (2 John 1:8-9). What could that person lose besides her salvation?

Jesus told John the apostle to write to the angel of the church of Ephesus, "Nevertheless I have *somewhat* against thee, because thou hast left thy first love. Remember therefore from whence thou art fallen, and repent, and do the first works; or else I will come unto thee quickly, and will remove thy candlestick out of his place, except thou repent" (Rev. 2:4-5).

Jesus told John to write to the angel of the church in Sardis, "He that overcometh, the same shall be clothed in white raiment; and I will not blot out his name out of the book of life, but I will confess his name before my Father, and before his angels" (Rev. 3:5). Whose name might not be blotted out of the "book of life?" The Christian. This tells us that if the Christian does not overcome his name will be blotted out. One has to be in the book of life before he can be blotted out.

Jesus told John to write to the angel of the church of the Laodiceans, "So then because thou art lukewarm, and neither cold nor hot, I will spue thee out of my mouth. Because thou sayest, I am rich, and increased with goods, and have need of nothing; and knowest not that thou art wretched, and miserable, and poor, and blind, and naked" (Rev. 3:16-17). Who might be spewed from the mouth of Jesus besides those who were with Him?

Of all false teachings that man has fabricated, except perhaps those of the Catholic and Mormon churches, this doctrine of once saved always saved must be the most absurd. In light of all the Bible has to say warning saved people to remain faithful, how could anyone believe that he cannot fall and be lost in hell if he sins continually and refuses to repent? It's ludicrous! It's not at all reasonable; even no human would behave that way, but the preacher expects God to. It's outrageous!

Some people argue that we cannot be lost after being saved because Paul said, "For I am persuaded, that neither death, nor life, nor angels, nor principalities, nor powers, nor things present, nor things to come, Nor height, nor depth, nor any other creature, shall be able to separate us from the love of God, which is in Christ Jesus our Lord" (Romans 8:38-39). Surely nothing can separate us from God's love, but this passage does not say that we cannot separate ourselves from God. God will keep us secure as long as we will let Him.

It's like a man drowning in a raging river calling for help. You help him, then he jumps back into the river again. He was saved but now he is lost again.

In explaining the parable of the tares to His disciples, Jesus described the scene at the end of the world. "The Son of man shall send forth his angels, and they shall gather out of his kingdom all things that offend, and them which do iniquity; And shall cast them into a furnace of fire: there shall be wailing and gnashing of teeth" (Matt 13:41-42). Jesus said this harvest is "the end of the world" in verses thirty-nine and forty. Those who "do iniquity" are in the kingdom along with the righteous, and will be cast out. Verse 41 says the wicked will be gathered "out of his kingdom."

The preacher has it wrong! What about those attending his church?

THE HOLY SPIRIT

BAPTISM, INDWELLING and MIRACLES

The preacher speculates a great deal about the Holy Spirit. But all we really know about the Holy Spirit is what we read in the Bible. Anything else is no more than a guess.

To be fair to the preacher, he is not alone. When we go back to the time of the life and teaching of Jesus, we see there were spiritual leaders who were wrong then, too. Only a few were willing to accept Jesus. The scribes and the priests should have known the Old Testament scriptures. Today, the preacher should know the scriptures; he has every opportunity. Do you suppose that many of them do know, but they are so wrapped up in church, family and friends that they just can't bring themselves around to breaking away from what they have held onto for so long? Anyone would find it hard to break away from all he'd ever known. Besides, everyone else seems to be believing and teaching false doctrine. But not everyone is.

It's hard to point out the preacher's errors and not sound critical or judgmental. But that's certainly not the intent here. This material is written hoping that someone will learn the truth and obey the gospel and become a Christian. Is it better to believe a preacher who is in error or to believe the Bible?

Now let's get with the subject at hand, the Holy Spirit. The preacher might tell you that you need to have the Holy Spirit fall on you before you can be saved. He might tell you that you have to be affected somehow by the Holy

Spirit after you are saved as evidence that you are saved. He might tell you that the Holy Spirit told him to do something like preach on a certain topic. He may have you believe that the Holy Spirit dwells in him personally and affects what he does and says. He may say the Holy Spirit brings peace or comforts him. He will have you believe the Holy Spirit will do these things for you, too, if you listen to his preaching.

The preacher will have you feel something as evidence that you're saved. The scriptures tell us that the Holy Spirit bears witness with our spirit that we are the children of God. We want to know how the Holy Spirit bears this witness. First, let's look at that passage: "The Spirit itself beareth witness with our spirit, that we are the children of God" (Romans 8:16). This satisfies our need to know if we truly are children of God. How does this work? The Spirit tells us what to do by the written Word. <u>This is His witness</u>. We compare what He said in the written Word to what we are doing. <u>This is our witness</u>. This is how His spirit bears witness with our spirit as to whether or not we are children of God.

In regards to this matter of having to feel something in order to know that we are saved. It's a very popular notion. There is a perfect example in the New Testament of a person who felt certain in his heart that he was pleasing God. That person was the Apostle Paul before he became a Christian. The preacher will say, "I know I'm saved, I feel it in my heart." While he says this he may place his hand over his heart. Paul was certain he was right with God while he was chasing Christians to have them jailed and sometimes even killed. He <u>felt</u> that he was right.

When we think we are right with God it is a pleasing feeling. When we feel certain we are right we feel really good. It's an especially good feeling when we know we were lost and now think we are saved. After Paul became a Christian, he said, "I have lived in all good conscience before God until this day" (Acts 23:1). Prior to his conversion he didn't know he was wrong, but he was. We simply cannot go by our feelings. There are other examples, but this is enough.

Suppose one feels right having been immersed in water for baptism, and another feels right having been sprinkled with water for baptism. Let's say the Bible teaches that only one form of baptism is acceptable. Both of our characters feel wonderful, just ready to jump out of their skin! We have a problem. One feels good, but he's wrong. He feels just as good as the other. This proves that you cannot go by what you feel. We feel a certain way depending on what we've been taught. (Of course, sprinkling is not baptism. Baptism, by definition, is immersion.)

The preacher will tell you that the Holy Spirit lives in him, that He personally dwells in him. He might call it a direct indwelling, a bodily indwelling, a personal indwelling or something of that sort, meaning the Holy Spirit is actually living in his body, under his skin. We'll compare this to the Bible.

We cannot say more than what the Bible says, unless we wish to speculate. A reasonable person will not rely on the preacher's speculation. Does the Holy Spirit live under the preacher's skin? Many preachers will tell you they have had Holy Spirit baptism. Have they? We'll see.

Before Jesus went back to heaven He told the apostles, among other things, that the Holy Spirit would come and bring to their remembrance the things that He had taught them and show them things to come. So the Holy Spirit was responsible for delivering to the apostles the Word which we now have written in the Bible. The Apostle John said, "it is the Spirit that beareth witness, because the Spirit is truth" (1 John 5:6). This is not to suggest that the Holy Spirit is not a distinct personality. He is one of three Persons in the God-Head.

To assure you of what Jesus said to the apostles before ascending into heaven, read John 14:16-17, and 26: "And I will pray the Father, and he shall give you another Comforter, that he may abide with you for ever; *Even* the Spirit of truth,...But the Comforter, *which is* the Holy Ghost, whom the Father will send in my name, he shall teach you all things, and bring all things to your remembrance, whatsoever I have said unto you." Chapter sixteen, verse thirteen says, "he will guide you into all truth" and "he will shew you things to come."

As we move through this study of the Holy Spirit, we learn what inspiration is. This is extremely important to us today because it assures us that what we read in the Bible did not come from man, but from God. There are at least three very important statements in the Bible that show us how inspiration works. Notice the phrase in Acts 1:16, "the Holy Ghost by the mouth of David spake." As we move to 2 Peter 1:20-21, as Peter was reminding people that "no prophecy of the scripture is of any private interpretation," he said, "For the prophecy came not in old time by the will of man: but holy men of God spake *as they were* moved by the Holy Ghost." And there's one more: "All scripture *is* given by inspiration of God" (II Tim3:16). The word "inspiration" means God breather.

It's reassuring to know that we can truly depend on what the Bible tells us, for Jesus said, "Heaven and earth shall pass away, but my words shall not pass away" (Matt. 24:35). And this written word was given to us by the Holy

Spirit through the mouths of the apostles. Jesus, as He was promising to send the Holy Spirit to the apostles said that they would be "endued with power from on high" (Luke 24:49). Notice the significance of this statement later.

There are two examples in the Bible of Holy Spirit baptism. The first example was on Pentecost in Acts, chapter two. The other is approximately ten years later at the house of a Gentile named Cornelius. Luke tells us in Acts ten, about it and then later in chapter eleven he records Peter's account of the event.

As we have seen, Jesus promised to send the Holy Spirit to the apostles. It's important to notice that the Holy Spirit was promised to only the apostles and to no one else. Remember, Luke wrote the gospel according to Luke, and he also wrote the Acts of the Apostles, the book of Acts. Luke took up in Acts where he left off in the book of Luke. At the end of Luke, he records a statement of Jesus, "I send the promise of my Father upon you: but tarry ye in the city of Jerusalem, until ye be endued with power from on high" (Luke 24:49). At the beginning of the book of Acts, Luke records that statement again, "And, being assembled together with *them*, commanded them that they should not depart from Jerusalem, but wait for the promise of the Father, which, *saith he*, ye have heard of me. For John truly baptized with water; but ye shall be baptized with the Holy Ghost not many days hence" (Acts 1:4-5), again, to only the apostles.

The "not many days hence" refers to the forty days from the time Jesus went back to heaven to Pentecost. Ten days had already passed since the Passover celebration. "Penty" is from a word meaning fifty. Pentecost was fifty days after Passover. But the important thing here is that the apostles were going to "be baptized with the Holy Ghost." The promise was never made to anyone else.

Peter told people how to receive the <u>gift</u> of the Holy Ghost in Acts 2:38: "Peter said unto them, Repent, and be baptized every one of you in the name of Jesus Christ for the remission of sins, and ye shall receive the gift of the Holy Ghost." But there's a difference between the baptism of the Holy Ghost and the gift of the Holy Ghost, as we shall see when we learn what was special about the baptism of the Holy Ghost.

Jesus told a woman from Samaria to give Him a drink of water. She wanted to know how it was that a Jew asked her for water. Jesus told her, "If thou knewest the gift of God, and who it is that saith to thee, Give me to drink; thou wouldest have asked of him, and he would have given thee living water" (John 4:10). This verse talks about a gift of God. Paul told the Ephesians, "unto every one of us is given grace according to the measure of the gift of Christ" (Eph. 4:7). So there is also a gift of Christ. Why should anyone speculate about the gift of the Holy Ghost? Is the gift of the Holy Spirit any more special than the gift of God or the gift of Christ?

What is it to be baptized? Better asked, what is it to be immersed? If you are immersed in something you are overwhelmed or inundated by it, or submerged into it. If the word had been translated into English rather than transliterated, it would say "immerse" rather than "baptize." The apostles were immersed in the Holy Spirit. Are we baptized in God or Christ like the apostles were baptized in the Holy Spirit? No. So the gift of the Holy Spirit is different from the baptism of the Holy Spirit.

Now the preacher will argue that the one hundred and twenty mentioned in Acts 1:15, were all baptized with the

73

Holy Spirit. But he's wrong. Follow the nouns and pronouns in the record starting in Acts chapter one, and you will see that only the apostles received the baptism of the Holy Spirit. The "apostles" in Acts 1:2, is the noun. "They" is the pronoun used from there on when Jesus was talking about people receiving the baptism of the Holy Ghost. "Apostles" is the antecedent of the pronoun "they." So it's easy to see that only the apostles received the baptism of the Holy Spirit. Besides, when we see how the Holy Spirit baptism affected or influenced the apostles and no others we conclude that only they received that baptism. Notice, too, that those preaching on the day of Pentecost were all from Galilee. It's not likely that all one hundred and twenty present that day were from Galilee.

Notice, also, that Peter stood up with the eleven (other apostles), not the one hundred and twenty, to preach on Pentecost. "But Peter, standing up with the eleven, lifted up his voice, and said unto them, Ye men of Judaea, and all *ye* that dwell at Jerusalem, be this known unto you, and hearken to my words" (Acts 2:14). And they began to preach.

Jesus repeated the promise of the Holy Spirit to the apostles immediately before going back into heaven. "But ye shall receive power, after that the Holy Ghost is come upon you: and ye shall be witnesses unto me both in Jerusalem, and in all Judaea, and in Samaria, and unto the uttermost part of the earth. And when he had spoken these things, while they beheld, he was taken up; and a cloud received him out of their sight" (Acts 1:8-9).

Notice that baptism of the Holy Spirit had nothing to do with the salvation of the apostles. The preacher today, if he is a true Calvinist, will tell you that you can't even believe or understand the Bible unless the Holy Spirit first falls on you. The Holy Spirit baptism enabled the

74

apostles to teach lessons they had never studied. It enabled them to speak languages they had never learned. Holy Spirit baptism enabled the apostles to perform miracles. The apostles had the power to pass on the powers of the Holy Spirit to others by laying their hands on them. But the recipient of those powers were not able to pass the powers to others.

To prove this last point, we look at Acts 6:5-6, to learn that a man named Philip was among several men who had the apostles' hands laid on them that they might receive the Holy Spirit. This enabled them to perform miracles. In Acts chapter eight, Philip was in Samaria preaching and performing miracles. Philip was not an apostle. "Now when the apostles which were at Jerusalem heard that Samaria had received the word of God, they sent unto them Peter and John: Who, when they were come down, prayed for them, that they might receive the Holy Ghost: (For as yet he was fallen upon none of them: only they were baptized in the name of the Lord Jesus.) Then laid they *their* hands on them, and they received the Holy Ghost" (Acts 8:14-17) (Emphasis is mine). Philip could not lay hands on the people of Samaria to enable them to perform miracles. They had to wait for the apostles to do that.

There was a man among the converts in Samaria, named Simon, who wanted the power the apostles had and offered to pay for it: "when Simon saw that through laying on of the apostles' hands the Holy Ghost was given, he offered them money, Saying, Give me also this power, that on whomsoever I lay hands, he may receive the Holy Ghost" (Acts 8:18-19). It cannot be emphasized enough that this was the only way others besides the apostles could receive the Holy Ghost.

So when Peter told the crowd in Acts 2:38, "Repent, and be baptized every one of you in the name of Jesus Christ for the remission of sins, and ye shall receive the gift of the Holy Ghost" (Acts 2:38-39), that gift of the Holy Ghost was not the same thing the apostles had, and it was not the same thing that Philip had. Philip, remember, was one who had the apostles' hands laid on him. It was not Holy Spirit baptism. Many others besides Philip had apostles' hands laid on them during the life of the apostles. This enabled them to perform miracles. Acts 2:38-39 is not promising Holy Spirit baptism.

There is a great deal of discussion about what the gift of the Holy Spirit is. Many Bible scholars understand it to mean what the Holy Spirit has to give. We know it's not what the apostles had or what Philip had because those people Philip preached to didn't have what the apostles or Philip had, yet they were Christians, and they had the gift of the Holy Ghost as was promised by Peter in Acts 2:38. There Peter said the promise of remission of sins and the gift of the Holy Ghost were promised to all who repent and are baptized. "For the promise is unto you, and to your children, and to all that are afar off, *even* as many as the Lord our God shall call" (Acts 2:39). The Christians at Samaria could not perform miracles until an apostle laid hand on them. And Christians today cannot perform miracles since there are no apostles to lay hands on them.

Before leaving Peter's sermon, notice that the apostles were talking to a crowd of at least 3,000, because that many obeyed the gospel, and these people were from 15 different nations (Acts 2:8-11). They heard the apostles speak in tongues. But these tongues were different from what the preacher today does. The apostles were speaking in languages (in tongues) all those people understood. "And how hear we every man in our own

76

tongue, wherein we were born?" (Acts 2:8). It was not the gibberish we hear today, it was different languages.

As mentioned earlier there was a Gentile, named Cornelius who was also baptized in the Holy Spirit. Cornelius was "A devout *man*, and one that feared God with all his house, which gave much alms to the people, and prayed to God always" (Acts 10:2). Even though about ten years had passed, the Jewish Christians were not ready to spread the Word to the Gentiles. It looks like those Jewish Christians thought they were still special. They needed to be shown somehow that the Gentiles should have the Gospel, even though Jesus had told the apostles to "Go ye into all the world, and preach the gospel to every creature. He that believeth and is baptized shall be saved" (Mark 16:15-16).

In the sermon on Pentecost, Peter mentioned a prophecy of Joel, in the Old Testament. And he said what's happening before you today is in fulfillment of Joel's prophesy. "And it shall come to pass afterward, *that* I will pour out my spirit upon all flesh; and your sons and your daughters shall prophesy, your old men shall dream dreams, your young men shall see visions" (Joel 2:28). All flesh was to have the Holy Spirit poured out on it. He said "all flesh." Did he mean everybody? In the Bible there were only two kinds of flesh, Jewish and Gentile flesh. Did he mean saint and sinner alike? No. Did he mean animal flesh? No. He meant the only kinds of flesh there were, Jewish and Gentile. You see, to the Jew when Joel prophesied, this is exactly what they understood, because at the time only Jewish flesh was chosen by God. They knew that Joel was referring to Jewish flesh and Gentile flesh when he said what he did.

Cornelius was of Gentile flesh. God chose him to be the one to convince the Jews that Gentile flesh was now acceptable to God. Cornelius was told to send for Peter. Peter saw a vision that convinced him to go. When he got to Cornelius' house he began to preach. While he preached the Holy Spirit fell on Cornelius and the others who heard Peter. As evidence that the Holy Spirit had fallen on them, Peter and the others who had come with him from Joppa heard Cornelius and his household "speak with tongues, and magnify God. Then answered Peter, Can any man forbid water, that these should not be baptized, which have received the Holy Ghost as well as we?" (Acts 10:46-47) Verse 48 says "he commanded them to be baptized." So now, the Holy Spirit had fallen on all flesh, both Jewish and Gentile.

Peter had to explain to the Christians at Jerusalem what had happened. So he related the whole thing to them, saying, for one thing, "And as I began to speak, the Holy Ghost fell on them, as on us at the beginning" (Acts 11:15). This statement is significant for one reason. If the Holy Spirit fell on all who were converted, Peter, more than likely, would have said something like, the Holy Ghost fell on them like everybody else who has been converted. Instead, he had to go back about ten years to find an example of Holy Spirit baptism.

Look at one more proof regarding the necessity of the laying on of an apostle's hands before an individual could receive the power to perform miracles like Philip. Look at Romans 1:9-11: "For God is my witness, whom I serve with my spirit in the gospel of his Son, that without ceasing I make mention of you always in my prayers; Making request, if by any means now at length I might have a prosperous journey by the will of God to come unto you. For I long to see you, that I may impart unto you some spiritual gift, to the end ye may be established" (Emphasis is mine). This also tells us something about the reason for this action, that they "may be established." The church was still young and needed establishment.

The apostles received the Holy Spirit baptism so that they could perform miracles to prove that God endorsed their teaching, and so that they could have the Word to speak in the first place, as well as other things. Cornelius received the Holy Spirit baptism so the Jewish Christians would be convinced that Gentiles were now accepted by God. There is no longer any need for the Holy Spirit baptism because now we have the written Word (and, of course, we know that Gentiles are accepted by God).

Peter told those people at Pentecost to repent and be baptized for remission of sins and the gift of the holy Ghost. He went on to say, "For the promise is unto you, and to your children, and to all that are afar off, *even* as many as the Lord our God shall call" (Acts 2:39). That includes all of us today. We have a problem if there is such a thing as Holy Spirit baptism today because we learn in Ephesians 4:4-5, that there is only one baptism today. *"There is* one body, and one Spirit, even as ye are called in one hope of your calling; One Lord, one faith, one baptism." You see, by the time Paul wrote to the Ephesians the two instances of Holy Spirit baptism had already taken place. Paul said there is one baptism. Only one baptism is left, that's water baptism.

Now let's consider the matter of Holy Spirit indwelling. The Holy Spirit does dwell in us, but not like the preacher says. How does the Holy Spirit dwell in us? Before we go further, look at some other Personalities that dwell in us, as well as other things that dwell in us.

"God is love; and he that dwelleth in love dwelleth in God, and God in him" (1 John 4:16). So, God dwells in us, and, by the way, we dwell in Him.

There are numerous places in the Bible that say Christ dwells in us. Let's look at just a couple. Jesus said, "He that eateth my flesh, and drinketh my blood, dwelleth in me, and I in him" (John 6:56). Jesus also said, "I am the vine, ye *are* the branches: He that abideth in me, and I in him, the same bringeth forth much fruit" (John 15:5).

As we study further, we learn that Christ dwells in us by faith. Look at Eph. 3:14-17: "For this cause I bow my knees unto the Father of our Lord Jesus Christ, . . That Christ may dwell in your hearts by faith." Not only does Christ dwell in us by faith, but also God the Father and the Holy Spirit dwell in us by faith. And that faith comes by the Word of God. "So then faith *cometh* by hearing, and hearing by the word of God" (Romans 10:17). 1 John 5:6 tells us the Spirit bears witness, "because the Spirit is truth."

There are other things that dwell in us besides the Persons of the Godhead: truth (2 John 1:1-2), faith (2 Tim. 1:5), love (1 John 3:17), eternal life (1 John 3:15), and even sin can dwell in us (Romans 7:16-17).

Back when Jesus promised the Apostles that the Holy Spirit would come, He called the spirit "the Spirit of truth" (John 16:13). It is through the truth that the Holy Spirit dwells in us. The Truth is the Word. The Word is the Faith, the body of doctrine which we believe. Paul called the Word the "sword of the Spirit." He said, "And take the helmet of salvation, and the sword of the Spirit, which is the word of God" (Eph. 6:17).

Heb. 4:12 says, "For the word of God *is* quick, and powerful, and sharper than any twoedged sword, piercing even to the dividing asunder of soul and spirit, and of the joints and marrow, and *is* a discerner of the thoughts and intents of the heart." Remember a statement of Paul's,

"For I am not ashamed of the gospel of Christ: for it is the power of God unto salvation to every one that believeth; to the Jew first, and also to the Greek" (Romans 1:16).

The Holy Ghost dwells in us by the Word. The Word is the faith, the body of doctrine. So it is safe to say that the Holy Ghost dwells in us by faith or by the word. The preacher has it wrong again.

Closely associated with the baptism of the Holy Spirit was the ability to perform miracles. Do miracles take place today? No, for one thing the purpose for miracles has passed. And, of course, there are no longer any apostles to perform them, or to pass on the ability to perform them.

There is such a thing as God's providence; otherwise there would be no reason to petition God in prayer. God answers prayers using natural means. But miracles require unnatural means. With a miracle God intervened in the natural.

Someone who could perform miracles could also raise the dead. Let the modern-day miracle performer try that. It doesn't matter how many times you hear the preacher claim to have experienced a miracle, don't believe him. It just didn't happen! Two passages will prove it.

By suggesting that miracles have ceased because the purposes for them have ceased requires a look at the passages that tell us about those purposes. Miracles could be performed by Christ, of course, then by the apostles, and by those on whom the apostles laid their hands.

Look first at the purpose of miracles Jesus performed. "And many other signs truly did Jesus in the presence of his disciples, which are not written in this book: But these are written, that ye might believe that Jesus is the Christ" (John 20:30-31). Today, belief (or faith) comes by hearing God's Word, as we saw in Romans 1:16.

One purpose of the apostle's miracles was to show that God endorsed their teachings. "How shall we escape, if we neglect so great salvation; which at the first began to be spoken by the Lord, and was confirmed unto us by them that heard *him*; God also bearing *them* witness, both with signs and wonders, and with divers miracles, and gifts of the Holy Ghost, according to his own will?" (Heb. 2:3-4). Another reason that the apostles performed miracles was so that their hearers "faith should not stand in the wisdom of men, but in the power of God" (1 Cor. 2:4-5). One more reason the apostles performed miracles was that their ability to perform miracles was "Truly the signs of an apostle were wrought among you in all patience, in signs, and wonders, and mighty deeds" (2 Cor. 12:12).

We learn something in 1 Cor. 14:22, about why those on whom the apostles laid hands, could perform miracles. "Wherefore tongues are for a sign, not to them that believe, but to them that believe not: but prophesying *serveth* not for them that believe not, but for them which believe." As we move to Ephesians chapter four, we see that part of the reason the hands-laid-on group performed miracles, was to help the church grow from infancy to maturity.

Ephesians four is one place we learn that miracles are no longer needed. Parts of Ephesians four are quoted here. You might like to read the whole short chapter in your Bible. Since you have access to the whole chapter in your Bible, it seems not to do it injustice to quote only the highlights here.

"I therefore, ..., beseech you that ye walk worthy of the vocation ...Endeavouring to keep the unity of the Spirit.... *There is* one body, and one Spirit, ...one hope ...One Lord, one faith, one baptism, One God ...But unto every one of us is given grace according to the measure of the gift of Christ. ... When he ascended up on high, he ...gave gifts unto men. . . .he gave some, apostles; and some, prophets; and some, evangelists; and some, pastors and teachers; For the perfecting of the saints... Till we all come in the unity of the faith, and of the knowledge of the Son of God, unto a perfect man,...: That we *henceforth* be no more children, ...But speaking the truth in love, may grow up into him in all things, ...From whom the whole body fitly joined together and compacted by that which every joint supplieth, according to the effectual working in the measure of every part ..." (Eph. 4:1-16).

Here Paul uses the figure of a child growing up to become a full grown man. The church, in its infancy, needed the gifts that Christ gave to it when He ascended into heaven. These gifts were given so the church would be complete even from the start. The word "perfect" suggests completeness. These miraculous gifts were given so the church could, as stated in verse thirteen, come in the unity of the faith, and of the knowledge of the Son of God.

Notice, in verse eight, of Ephesians four, Paul said when Jesus ascended on high He gave gifts unto men. In 1 Cor. 13:8, he says the same thing. So the two passages are talking about the same thing. In chapter twelve, of I Corinthians, Paul gave a list of miraculous gifts. "And God hath set some in the church, first apostles, secondarily prophets, thirdly teachers, after that miracles, then gifts of healings, helps, governments, diversities of tongues."

Paul follows this list with some words of admonition

"covet earnestly the best gifts: and yet shew I unto you a more excellent way," verse 31. That more excellent way is described in the first few verses of chapter thirteen. That more excellent way is love. Here we find one of the most beautiful passages in the Bible. To summarize, Paul says that he could have the best of gifts and still he would be nothing without love. In the King James Version the word "charity" is used. Newer versions use the word "love."

Read verse eight of I Corinthians thirteen: "Charity never faileth: but whether *there be* prophecies, they shall fail; whether *there be* tongues, they shall cease; whether *there be* knowledge, it shall vanish away." Love will last after the miraculous gifts are gone. "Charity never faileth" but prophecies, tongues and miraculous knowledge would cease. He's not talking about some time in our future. He's talking about the time when the church grew to maturity or completeness.

"For we know in part, and we prophesy in part. But when that which is perfect is come, then that which is in part shall be done away." (vs 9-10). The scriptures were not yet delivered completely. In other words, the Bible was still being developed. Until then these gifts were necessary. Look up the word originally translated "perfect" in this verse and you will find that it means complete. The scriptures need to be completed before the gifts were to be done away.

From here, Paul compares the completion of revelation to the development of a person. In this verse we see that when revelation was completed those "childish things," the miraculous gifts, were done away. "When I was a child, I spake as a child, I understood as a child, I thought as a child: but when I became a man, I put away childish things" (v 11).

"For now we see through a glass, darkly; but then face to face: now I know in part; but then shall I know even as also I am known" (v 12).

"And now abideth faith, hope, charity, these three; but the greatest of these *is* charity" (v13). This tells us that after the miraculous gifts are gone these three, faith, hope and charity will still be around. One reason charity, or love, is the greatest of these three is because at the end of time there will no longer be need for faith or hope. Faith is the substance of things for which we hope (Heb. 11:1). And hope is our desire and expectation. Our faith and hope will last until Christ comes back, then we will no longer just believe or just hope; that which is believed and hoped for will be real. But love will continue on into eternity.

Go back to Ephesians four, for one last thought regarding the reason for the gifts. "That we *henceforth* be no more children, tossed to and fro, and carried about with every wind of doctrine, by the sleight of men, *and* cunning craftiness, whereby they lie in wait to deceive; But speaking the truth in love" (Eph. 4:14-15). This should remind us of the preacher. He's wrong in respect to these things taught by the apostle Paul.

Yes, the preacher has it wrong!

WHAT HAPPENS AT THE SECOND COMING OF CHRIST?

Man's imagination has gone wild! Some of the most spectacular imaginations of man concern the second coming of Christ. Folks expect to fight. Some expect Jesus to set up a kingdom and reign in Jerusalem. Some expect what they call a rapture. The Bible says nothing about a fight when Jesus comes back. The Bible says nothing about Him setting up a kingdom when He comes back. The Bible says absolutely nothing about a rapture. Even the ideas used to support the theory of a rapture are confusing and they are not supported in any way by the Bible. These ideas come from a misunderstanding of the Bible. It's not hard, though, to see what will happen when Jesus comes again if all the scriptures relating to His coming are considered. And it's important to not bring in passages that do not relate to that event.

First, never start Bible study trying to prove something. Honesty requires that we study to learn and to benefit from the study. To be successful bring in all passages that relate to a topic and nothing else.

When the preacher speculates about the next coming of Christ he misuses passages like some found in the book of Daniel, Matthew 24, and the book of Revelation. There is no attempt here to completely exhaust the meanings of the relevant passages found in these books, but a quick look at each will be enough to make the necessary point.

In the book of Daniel, Daniel interpreted a dream of Nebuchadnezzar, king of Babylon. (For a full account read Daniel two.) In his dream, Nebuchadnezzar had seen an image of what must have looked to him like a statue. "This image's head *was* of fine gold, his breast and his arms of silver, his belly and his thighs of brass, His legs of iron, his feet part of iron and part of clay. Thou sawest till that a stone was cut out without hands, which smote the image upon his feet *that were* of iron and clay, and brake them to pieces" (Dan. 2:32-34).

Daniel explained the meaning of the dream. "Thou *art* this head of gold. And after thee shall arise another kingdom inferior to thee, and another third kingdom of brass, which shall bear rule over all the earth. And the fourth kingdom shall be strong as iron: forasmuch as iron breaketh in pieces and subdueth all *things*: and as iron that breaketh all these, shall it break in pieces and bruise" (Dan. 2:38-40).

So we have four kingdoms. Before finishing the book of Daniel we learn that the kingdom of the Meads and Persians follow the kingdom of Nebuchadnezzar. In our study of history we learn that the Greeks under Alexander the Great formed the third kingdom. Then came the Roman Empire. During the days of these kings a kingdom would come that would last forever. "And in the days of these kings shall the God of heaven set up a kingdom, which shall never be destroyed: and the kingdom shall not be left to other people, *but* it shall break in pieces and consume all these kingdoms, and it shall stand for ever" (Dan. 2:44).

This is another place where the preacher has it wrong. He agrees that Jesus was supposed to set up a kingdom during the time of the Roman Empire, but He failed. Of course, we know that God cannot fail. Jesus did set up a kingdom; it was a spiritual kingdom, and it shall last forever. We shall see later that when the end comes Jesus will deliver that kingdom up to God the Father.

Significantly, Daniel prophesied that when Jesus should go back to heaven (now, two thousand years ago) is when He was to receive that kingdom. "I saw in the night visions, and, behold, *one* like the Son of man came with the clouds of heaven, and came to the Ancient of days, and they brought him near before him. And there was given him dominion, and glory, and a kingdom" (Dan. 7:13-14). The Ancient of days here refers to God the Father. When Jesus went back to God (the Ancient of days) the first time is when He received that kingdom.

At one point in the book of Daniel, he referred to the "last days." In that reference he is speaking of the last days of the Old Testament system of religious practice. We see that phrase often in the Old Testament where it always refers to that point in time when the Jews would no longer be dealt with differently from the Gentiles. Under the New Testament no distinction is made between Jew and Gentile. "There is neither Jew nor Greek, there is neither bond nor free, there is neither male nor female: for ye are all one in Christ Jesus" (Gal. 3:28).

Though the preacher applies several Old Testament passages to the end of time, he simply has it wrong. These in Daniel and all other Old Testament passages referring to the coming kingdom, were referring to Christ's first coming and establishing a spiritual kingdom, which He did.

Jesus is not coming back to set up a physical kingdom in Jerusalem. There is, in fact, nothing special about the Jews any more. Paul said, "For there is no difference between the Jew and the Greek: for the same Lord over all is rich unto all that call upon him" (Romans 10:12). The kingdom was never intended to be a physical kingdom. Jesus said, ". . .My kingdom is not of this world: if my kingdom were of this world, then would my servants fight" (John 18:36). He also said, . . .The kingdom of God cometh not with observation: Neither shall they say, Lo here! or, lo there! for, behold, the kingdom of God is within you." (Luke 17:20-21).

Every prophecy in the Old Testament referring to the Jews as a distinct people has been fulfilled. Every Old Testament promise that God made to the Jews that relate to their possession of the land of Palestine has been fulfilled. "And the Lord gave unto Israel all the land which he sware to give unto their fathers; and they possessed it, and dwelt therein. And the Lord gave them rest round about, according to all that he sware unto their fathers: and there stood not a man of all their enemies before them; the Lord delivered all their enemies into their hand. There failed not ought of any good thing which the Lord had spoken unto the house of Israel; all came to pass" (Josh. 21:43-45). God gave them everything He promised but they were unfaithful and lost it. The return of Jews to Israel in 1948 is not a fulfillment of any Bible prophecy.

Now let's consider briefly Matthew 24, which the preacher perverts to get many of his false ideas. The temple in Jerusalem must have been a marvelous structure. It was so beautiful that even as many times as Jesus had seen it, His disciples, as they walked away from it, must have said to Jesus something like, Just look; look at this wonderful building (verse 1). Jesus replied, "See ye not all these things? verily I say unto you, There shall not be left here one stone upon another, that shall not be thrown down" (Matt. 24:2). The disciples wanted to know more, so they asked, "Tell us, when shall these things be? and what *shall be* the sign of thy coming, and of the end of the world" (Matt. 24:3)?

The disciples might not have known it, but they asked two questions. Question number one (1): when would the temple be destroyed, and question two (2): what

89

would be a sign of His returning and the end of the world. Jesus answered the first question in verses five through thirty four. He answers the second question starting in verse thirty six. Regarding the end of the world He said, "But of that day and hour knoweth no *man,* no, not the angels of heaven, but my Father only. But as the days of Noe *were,* so shall also the coming of the Son of man be" (Matt. 24:36-37). Jesus gave signs of the coming of the destruction of the temple (question one), but no signs were given for the end of the world (second question) only the Father knows that (verse 36). This proves the signs in verses five through thirty-four refer to something besides the end of the world. All of those "signs of the times" were to take place before the destruction of Jerusalem and the temple. This destruction took place in A.D. Seventy. Importantly, Jesus said in verse 34, "This generation shall not pass, till all these things be fulfilled.

Why do you suppose the disciples asked the questions the way they did? Why do you suppose they connected the destruction of the temple with the end of the world, which apparently they did? The reason is they thought that when the temple was destroyed surely that must mean the end of the world.

The Jews had been so rebellious and disobedient that God was going to visit upon them total destruction from off the land He had given to their ancestors. This visitation is specifically the "coming" of the "Son of man" mentioned in verses 27 through 31, of Matthew twenty-four. This visitation was symbolic the same as the "comings" (visitations) were in the Old Testament. We know this is so because of what Jesus said in verse thirty-four: "Verily I say unto you, This generation shall not pass, till all these things be fulfilled." (If anyone wants to argue about the meaning of the word "generation," it means the same here that it does

90

everywhere else in the Bible. Jesus meant those living at that time.) So, everything foretold up to verse thirty-three was to take place before the destruction of the temple in A.D Seventy.

The meaning of this visitation and "the stars shall fall from heaven," etc. may not be easy to accept at first until we look back to see how such phrases were used in the Old Testament. The Jews at the time of Jesus probably were familiar with those kinds of phrases. These statements simply meant that something bad was going to happen. And something really bad was going to happen, Jerusalem and the temple were going to be destroyed.

Notice the language used in these three Old Testament passages. "For the stars of heaven and the constellations thereof shall not give their light: the sun shall be darkened in his going forth, and the moon shall not cause her light to shine" (Isaiah 13:10). Isaiah was speaking of the destruction of Babylon. "The sun and the moon shall be darkened, and the stars shall withdraw their shining" (Joel 3:15). "The sun shall be turned into darkness, and the moon into blood, before the great and the terrible day of the Lord come" (Joel 2:31). Joel was prophesying the destruction of Jerusalem. We know this is so because both he and Jesus said nothing worse had ever happened before or ever would happen again after this event. This statement cannot be made about two different events.

When reading Joel's statement and that of Jesus, it is easy to see that they were talking about the same event. Joel said, "A day of darkness and of gloominess, a day of clouds and of thick darkness, as the morning spread upon the mountains: a great people and a strong; there hath not been ever the like, neither shall be any more after it, *even* to the years of many generations" (Joel 2:2).

91

Jesus said, "For then shall be great tribulation, such as was not since the beginning of the world to this time, no, nor ever shall be" (Matt. 24:21).

Consider these Old Testament phrases; see if they are not like the ones used by Jesus to indicate swift destruction, a true visit from God: "the Lord rideth upon a swift cloud, and shall come into Egypt" (Isaiah 19:1). "so shall the Lord of hosts come down to fight for mount Zion" (Isaiah 31:4). "fear not: behold, your God will come *with* vengeance" (Isaiah 35:4). "behold, the Lord will come with fire, and with his chariots" (Isaiah 66:15). Of course, God was not literally in Egypt to fight. He was not speaking of actually coming physically.

It's no stretch of the imagination; the point is made. Verses twenty-seven through thirty-one of Matthew twenty-four, like those Old Testament passages, were used to emphasize the fact that bad things were going to happen. The "Son of man" was not going to make a personal, literal, physical visit.

The preacher might argue that these "signs of the times" must refer to the end of the world because Jesus said in Matthew 24:14, "And this gospel of the kingdom shall be preached in all the world for a witness unto all nations; and then shall the end come." But the gospel was preached to all the world before Jerusalem was destroyed. Paul said, "If ye continue in the faith grounded and settled, and *be* not moved away from the hope of the gospel, which ye have heard, *and* which was preached to every creature which is under heaven" Col. 1:23). And speaking of the apostles who were also called preachers, Paul said, "their sound went into all the earth, and their words unto the ends of the world" (Romans 10:18).

Ask the preacher why Jesus advised, "let them which be in Judaea flee into the mountains" (Matt. 24:14-16). There would be no hope of hiding in the mountains if He had been talking about the end of time. No body's going to make it to the mountains when Jesus returns. But they might have made it to the mountains before the Romans marched in to destroy the city of Jerusalem.

Matthew 24 doesn't lend any support whatsoever to those who wish to teach that Jesus is coming back for a rapture, to fight, to set up a kingdom, or any of those kinds of things.

Now consider the book of Revelation. First look at two passages; they are particularly significant:

"The Revelation of Jesus Christ, which God gave unto him, to shew unto his servants things which must shortly come to pass; and he sent and signified it by his angel unto his servant John" (Rev. 1:1). "And he said unto me, These sayings *are* faithful and true: and the Lord God of the holy prophets sent his angel to shew unto his servants the things which must shortly be done" (Rev. 22:6). (Emphasis is mine.) This Revelation is the most misunderstood book in the New Testament. But it's easy enough to understand these two passages. John was told to write about things which were going to happen soon. "Shortly" meant right away after his writing the letter, not two thousand years later! And he was told to put his words in signs (sign-ified). They were signified. They were symbolic, not literal. So the thousand year reign, along with the rest of the book, was put in signs and symbols. John made one of those statements about these events happening soon at the beginning of the book and the other at the end of the book. He wanted to be sure it was not misunderstood.

93

The chapter twenty of the book of Revelation, which is misused by the preacher to teach the false doctrines concerning the kingdom of Christ, says nothing about the second coming of Christ, a bodily resurrection, a reign on earth, a literal throne of David, Jerusalem, Christ on earth, or even us on earth.

First Corinthians 15:24 shows, in fact, that when Jesus does come back, He will deliver the kingdom to the Father. "Then *cometh* the end, when he shall have delivered up the kingdom to God, even the Father; when he shall have put down all rule and all authority and power." Paul goes on to say, "For he must reign, till he hath put all enemies under his feet. The last enemy *that* shall be destroyed *is* death" (1 Cor. 15:25-26).

Once more the preacher has it wrong!

So, nothing in the book of Daniel, Mathew 24, or the Book of Revelation says anything about Jesus coming back to set up a kingdom. These explanations may not be enough to convince some. But when we look at passages that really do pertain to the end of the world, these explanations will be more than convincing.

What does the Bible say about the second coming of Christ?

Watch, as you read the passages quoted in the next few pages, for proof that when Jesus comes back there will be the judgment day and everyone will go to his eternal reward or punishment as the case may be. Nothing more! And it will all take place on the last day.

"And when he had spoken these things, while they beheld, he was taken up; and a cloud received him out of their sight. And while they looked stedfastly toward heaven as he went up, behold, two men stood by them in white apparel; Which also said, Ye men of Galilee, why stand ye gazing up into heaven? this same Jesus, which is taken up from you into heaven, shall so come in like manner as ye have seen him go into heaven" (Acts 1:9-11). If Jesus comes as He went, He will not be dripping with blood, with a sword in His mouth, and with fire in His eyes as some may imagine that Revelation chapter nineteen teaches.

The following three passages say the righteous will be raised the last day, not before a rapture or before a literal 1,000 year reign on earth. "And this is the will of him that sent me, that every one which seeth the Son, and believeth on him, may have everlasting life: and I will raise him up at the last day" (John 6:40). "No man can come to me, except the Father which hath sent me draw him: and I will raise him up at the last day" (John 6:44). "Whoso eateth my flesh, and drinketh my blood, hath eternal life; and I will raise him up at the last day" (John 6:54). There is no time after the last day for a 1,000 year reign! It's impossible for there to be a thousand years worth of days after the last day.

The wicked will also be judged on the last day. "He that rejecteth me, and receiveth not my words, hath one that judgeth him: the word that I have spoken, the same shall judge him in the last day" (John 12:48). So, there's not going to be time for all the armies of the earth to gather in Megiddo to fight. This news will disappoint the preacher, because it takes away much of the sensational dogma he has been teaching his followers. Why would Christians wish to fight and kill the people during a thousand year reign that they are trying to help save today?

A favorite passage every preacher should be able to quote from memory teaches that the Lord will take His disciples

95

off the earth to be where He is, not come to earth where they are. He's simply coming back to get them. "Let not your heart be troubled: ye believe in God, believe also in me. In my Father's house are many mansions: if *it were* not *so*, I would have told you. I go to prepare a place for you. And if I go and prepare a place for you, I will come again, and receive you unto myself; that where I am, *there* ye may be also" (John 14:1-3). The Bible nowhere says Jesus will step foot on earth. The righteous will meet Him in the air. "Then we which are alive *and* remain shall be caught up together with them in the clouds, to meet the Lord in the air: and so shall we ever be with the Lord" (1 Thess 4:17)

"I charge *thee* therefore before God, and the Lord Jesus Christ, who shall judge the quick and the dead at his appearing and his kingdom" (2 Tim. 4:1). "At his appearing" there will be the judgment, not the establishment of a kingdom or a reign for 1,000 years before the judgment. He will judge the quick (living) and the dead "at his coming."

Read in your Bible I Cor. 15:22-28 and 50-54. Parts are quoted here: ". . . in Christ shall all be made alive. . . . at His coming. Then cometh the end, when he shall have delivered up the kingdom to God, even the Father, when he shall have put down all rule and all authority and power. For he must reign, till he hath put all enemies under his feet. The last enemy *that* shall be destroyed *is* death." Notice the phrase "at His coming." It is then that He will give the kingdom to God, the Father, not after 1,000 years. It cannot be stressed enough that at His coming He will give the kingdom to His Father. It exists today; it is a spiritual kingdom,

Starting with verse 50, we see ". . . that flesh and blood cannot inherit the kingdom of God; . . . We shall not all sleep, but we shall all be changed, In a moment, in the twinkling of an eye, . . . and the dead shall be raised incorruptible, and we shall be changed. For this corruptible must put on incorruption, and this mortal *must* put on immortality. So when this corruptible shall have put on incorruption, and this mortal shall have put on immortality, then shall be brought to pass the saying that is written, Death is swallowed up in victory."

At that time ("at His coming") the human body of the living righteous will become immortal. Human flesh and blood cannot inherit the kingdom of God. Since flesh and blood cannot inherit the kingdom of God, it certainly cannot literally reign in a kingdom. Even at that point in time death will be conquered and men will not continue to die for another 1,000 years as the preacher says.

Matthew 13:24-43, is a lengthy reading. It is a parable about too many weeds to pull out of a growing crop without disturbing the crop, so they must be left until harvest. Then the weeds will be separated from the crop. The point of the parable is that people will be sorted, the good from the bad. The righteous will "shine forth as the sun in the kingdom of their Father" (it will then be His). For the unrighteous "there shall be wailing and gnashing of teeth." This harvest is described as "the end of the world" (verse 39).

When the Lord returns all those who are dead will be raised at the same time, as we have seen already. The living Christians will meet Jesus in the air with the dead righteous who are coming with Him (I Thes. 4:17).

It is not clear to us exactly at what point formal sentencing will take place, or where we will stand before Jesus to be judged. But it is clear that we all will appear before Him to receive our reward whether it's good or bad.

97

Depending on the context from which passages are taken regarding Jesus' coming, we get certain information: He will return as He went (Acts 1:11). Angels will accompany the Lord when He returns (Matt. 25:31). All the dead will be raised at the same time, both saints and sinners (John 5:28-29). No one, except God the Father, knows when Jesus will return (II Peter3:10). He is coming to judge mankind (Heb. (9:27). The dead, God will bring with Him, indicating that they will be alive and raised from the dead (1 Thess. 4:14). The righteous who are alive will meet the Lord in the air to be with Him forever (1 Thess. 4:17). The earth will be destroyed (2 Peter 3:10-11). (All these scriptures are quoted elsewhere in this chapter.)

Nothing anywhere in the Bible says that Jesus will set up a kingdom when He returns. But what about that thousand year reign the preacher says so much about? We read about a thousand year reign in Revelation chapter twenty. We also read in Revelation about beasts that had seven heads and ten horns, and beasts that can talk. The preacher wants to make the thousand year reign literal but the beasts figurative. He can't do that. Do you know that some of these people call themselves prophets?

The beasts are just as literal as the reign. Besides, if you look closely at Revelation 20:1-4, from where the preacher does his "prophesying," you will see that only people who have their heads cut off lived and reigned with Christ. That leaves the rest of us out. We know that Revelation was symbolic; it was put in signs and symbols. Those people, at the time John wrote, were living that stuff he talked about. It must have been easier for them to understand the book of Revelation than we can today. These things about which John wrote were going to happen soon.

Jesus said, "Marvel not at this: for the hour is coming, in the which all that are in the graves shall hear his voice, And shall come forth; they that have done good, unto the resurrection of life; and they that have done evil, unto the resurrection of damnation" (John 5:28-29). This "hour" about which Jesus spoke tells us that at a given point in time all the dead would be raised, both the saints and the sinners. It also says they will be judged at the same time. Today, the preacher says that is not so! The preacher wants you to believe that the saints will be raised then a thousand years later the sinners will be raised. What purpose would God have for this? Is it so we can fight over in Palestine? The preacher has a purpose for it. Not to judge the man, but it seems that he enjoys telling the tantalizing stories about a battle between saints and sinners, and all the other sensationalism that goes along with it.

Paul said there would be a resurrection of the dead, both of the just and unjust. "But this I confess unto thee, that after the way which they call heresy, so worship I the God of my fathers, believing all things which are written in the law and in the prophets: And have hope toward God, which they themselves also allow, that there shall be a resurrection of the dead, both of the just and unjust" (Acts 24:14-15). Here Paul stood before Felix as certain accusations were being made against him. The "they themselves" in this verse refers to the Pharisees in the crowd who also believed there would be a resurrection.

First Thess. 4:13-17 is quite long, but it is probably where the preacher gets his idea of a rapture. Of course, the idea is not here, neither is the word "rapture." "But I would not have you to be ignorant, brethren, concerning them which are asleep, that ye sorrow not, even as others which have no hope. For if we believe that Jesus died and rose again, even so them also which sleep in Jesus

99

will God bring with him. For this we say unto you by the word of the Lord, that we which are alive *and* remain unto the coming of the Lord shall not prevent (precede) them which are asleep. For the Lord himself shall descend from heaven with a shout, with the voice of the archangel, and with the trump of God: and the dead in Christ shall rise first: Then we which are alive *and* remain shall be caught up together with them in the clouds, to meet the Lord in the air: and so shall we ever be with the Lord."

In this letter to the Thessalonians, we learn that when the Lord returns the righteous shall be forever with Him in the air, off the earth, starting at the time of His coming, not 1,000 years later, and not after a seven year rapture. The phrase "are asleep" refers to those who are dead. Those people must have been concerned about others who die before the Lord returns. (In modern versions of the Bible the word "prevent" in verse fifteen is translated "precede.")

Peter said, "the day of the Lord will come as a thief in the night; in the which the heavens shall pass away with a great noise, and the elements shall melt with fervent heat, the earth also and the works that are therein shall be burned up." He goes on to say in verse twelve, "the heavens being on fire shall be dissolved, and the elements shall melt with fervent heat" (2 Peter 3:10-12). Peter's comment here may be the most profound statement in the Bible that tells us what will happen when Jesus returns. Notice the phrase "in the which." This phrase tells us that the very day the Lord comes, heaven and earth will melt. When this happens there will be no Jerusalem in which Christ could reign.

There is no thousand year period between the raising of Christians and all others. The preacher has it wrong!

100

Regarding the Judgment consider the next few passages:

"When the Son of man shall come in his glory, and all the holy angels with him, then shall he sit upon the throne of his glory: And before him shall be gathered all nations: and he shall separate them one from another, as a shepherd divideth *his* sheep from the goats: And he shall set the sheep on his right hand, but the goats on the left" (Matt. 25:31-33).

"And as it is appointed unto men once to die, but after this the judgment" (Heb. 9:27). Nothing else! Just our reward or our punishment follows.

"But why dost thou judge thy brother? or why dost thou set at nought thy brother? for we shall all stand before the judgment seat of Christ. For it is written, *As I live,* saith the Lord, every knee shall bow to me, and every tongue shall confess to God. So then every one of us shall give account of himself to God" (Romans 14:10-12).

"For we must all appear before the judgment seat of Christ; that every one may receive the things *done* in *his* body, according to that he hath done, whether *it be* good or bad" (2 Cor. 5:10).

Jesus will reign as King until He returns and conquers death. Death is conquered by the resurrection of the dead. And as we saw, when He has finished reigning, He will give the kingdom to God the Father. And the earth will be destroyed.

How much plainer can it be? Jesus said, "My kingdom is not of this world: if my kingdom were of this world, then would my servants fight, that I should not be delivered to the Jews: but now is my kingdom not from hence" (John

101

18:36). The kingdom of Christ is spiritual. We should be ecstatic to be a part of a kingdom of which Christ is King.

The preacher has it wrong.

CHURCH ORGANIZATION (AS IN THE BIBLE)

When the church was in its infancy it was necessary for some disciples to have special gifts.

In Eph. 4:8, 11-13, we read, "Wherefore he saith, When he ascended up on high, he led captivity captive, and gave gifts unto men. . . And he gave some, apostles; and some, prophets; and some, evangelists; and some, pastors and teachers; For the perfecting of the saints, for the work of the ministry, for the edifying of the body of Christ: Till we all come in the unity of the faith, and of the knowledge of the Son of God, unto a perfect man, unto the measure of the stature of the fulness of Christ." Notice he said, "Till we all come in the unity of the faith." As time passed by the church matured and came to the unity of the faith and to the knowledge of the Son of God. These miraculous gifts were to last only until then. Since the faith has been finished in the written Word these gifts are no longer needed. No one today receives miraculous gifts.

Referring to the same thing, Paul said in 1 Corinthians 13:10, "when that which is perfect is come, then that which is in part shall be done away." The word "perfect" in this verse and in Eph. 4:13 means complete. The word "perfecting" in Eph. 4:12 means complete furnishing. We no longer have prophets or apostles, but we do still have evangelists; pastors and teachers. These people in the church today do not need a miracle to become what they are, but they are still needed. Apostles and prophets are no longer needed; the Word is complete.

The Bible identifies only two offices in the church, the office of an elder or bishop, and the office of a deacon. The office of a bishop is mentioned in 1 Tim. 3:1: "This *is* a true saying, If a man desire the office of a bishop, he desireth a good work." The office of a deacon is

103

mentioned in 1 Tim. 3:10: "And let these also first be proved; then let them use the office of a deacon, being *found* blameless." The positions in the church of bishop and deacon are actually called "offices." <u>If man places other offices in the church, he does it without God's authority and without God's approval</u>.

When Paul wrote a letter to the Philippians, he addressed all those who constitute the church; the <u>saints</u>, <u>bishops</u> and <u>deacons</u>: "Paul and Timotheus, the servants of Jesus Christ, to all the saints in Christ Jesus which are at Philippi, with the bishops and deacons" (Phil. 1:1). "Saint" means sanctified, or set apart. People were sanctified in Old Testament times as well as now. "Moses went down from the mount unto the people, and sanctified the people" (Ex. 19:14). All sanctified people are saints, therefore, all Christians, since they are sanctified, are saints according to the scriptures. Would you pray to another Christian? Some people pray to other people whom they call saints. This is foreign to God's Word and contrary to His will. "For *there is* one God, and one mediator between God and men, the man Christ Jesus" (1 Tim 2:5).

Isaiah prophesied, "And the Gentiles shall see thy righteousness, and all kings thy glory: and thou shalt be called by a new name, which the mouth of the Lord shall name" (Isaiah 62:2). The preacher will tell you there is nothing in a name. The Apostle Peter doesn't agree with the preacher. He said, "Neither is there salvation in any other: for there is none other name under heaven given among men, whereby we must be saved" (Acts 4:12). God gave this new name! We are to wear Christ's name, Christian. The last part of Acts 11:26, says, "And the disciples were called Christians first in Antioch." Should we wear a name "under heaven given by men?" There are many names given by men today, and the preacher says that's alright.

The preacher will tell you it's okay to call him pastor. Preachers are not pastors in the Lord's church in most cases. If one is a pastor he has to meet certain qualifications. The same is true of deacons.

The qualifications of a pastor are identified in letters to Timothy and Titus. Look for the words, "elders," and "bishop" as you read these two short passages. You will not find the word "pastor" here, but that's who he's describing, as we shall see later.

"This *is* a true saying, If a man desire the office of a bishop, he desireth a good work. A bishop then must be blameless, the husband of one wife, vigilant, sober, of good behaviour, given to hospitality, apt to teach; Not given to wine, no striker, not greedy of filthy lucre; but patient, not a brawler, not covetous; One that ruleth well his own house, having his children in subjection with all gravity; (For if a man know not how to rule his own house, how shall he take care of the church of God?) Not a novice, lest being lifted up with pride he fall into the condemnation of the devil. Moreover he must have a good report of them which are without; lest he fall into reproach and the snare of the devil" (1 Tim. 3:1-7).

"For this cause left I thee in Crete, that thou shouldest set in order the things that are wanting, and ordain elders in every city, as I had appointed thee: If any be blameless, the husband of one wife, having faithful children not accused of riot or unruly. For a bishop must be blameless, as the steward of God; not selfwilled, not soon angry, not given to wine, no striker, not given to filthy lucre; But a lover of hospitality, a lover of good men, sober, just, holy, temperate; Holding fast the faithful word as he hath been taught, that he may be able by sound doctrine both to exhort and to convince the gainsayers" (Titus 1:5-9).

So, we see, for one thing, in these passages that the elder is the same as the bishop and this position in the church is called an office. How many so called pastors meet these qualifications?

Though the word "pastor" is not used in these texts, and the words "elders" and "bishop" are used, they refer to the same office as pastor. In Ephesians 4:11, where the word "pastors" is used, Young's Literal Translation uses the word "shepherds" instead of the word "pastors." The two words, "pastor" and "shepherd," come from the same original Greek word. In 1 Peter 5:1-2, Peter told the elders to feed the flock. "Feed," "pastor" and "shepherd" all come from the same root word. It's like telling a doctor to doctor, where the first "doctor" is a noun and the second "doctor" is a verb. He's telling the elders to elder. He's telling the elders to pastor. He could have told the pastors to pastor. The elder is called a shepherd or a pastor. In Titus 1:7, as we saw, the elder is called bishop. Paul calls the elders overseers in Acts 20:28, where he said, "the Holy Ghost hath made you overseers." One more term used to describe the same individual is "presbytery." "Neglect not the gift that is in thee, which was given thee by prophecy, with the laying on of the hands of the presbytery" (1 Tim. 4:14). The word "presbytery" means elders.

As further evidence that pastors are the same as elders or shepherds, in Acts 20:17, Paul called for the Ephesians elders to meet him: "And from Miletus he sent to Ephesus, and called the elders of the church." In the 28th verse, he told them to "Take heed therefore unto yourselves, and to all the flock, over the which the Holy

Ghost hath made you overseers, to feed the church of God." So, we see that elders are the same as overseers who are to tend or feed, shepherd or pastor, the flock.

More evidence is found in 1Peter 5:1-4, the elders (verse 1) were to "Feed the flock of God which is among you, taking the oversight *thereof*" (verse 2). So the elder is to take the oversight and feed or shepherd or pastor the flock.

The individual who holds this office is called elder, shepherd, bishop, presbytery, overseer, and pastor. In the Bible the preacher is never called pastor.

One thing that should be pointed out is the fact that there were always more than one elder in each congregation. Another is that the elders had authority to fulfill their duties only in the congregation of which they were members. Notice the instruction the Apostle Peter gave in 1 Peter 5:1-2: "The elders which are among you I exhort, who am also an elder, and a witness of the sufferings of Christ, and also a partaker of the glory that shall be revealed: Feed the flock of God which is among you, taking the oversight *thereof.*" The bishop has no authority outside the congregation of which he is a member. In the Lord's church there are no archbishops.

In the Lord's church there are no presidents, no counsels, no boards of directors, no cardinals, and no conventions to make church decisions. They are not needed. Christ is head of the church; He has given us His Word and it cannot be changed.

The other office mentioned is the office of deacon. Qualifications for deacons are found in 1 Tim. 3:8-12, "Likewise *must* the deacons *be* grave, not doubletongued, not given to much wine, not greedy of filthy lucre;

Holding the mystery of the faith in a pure conscience. And let these also first be proved; then let them use the office of a deacon, being *found* blameless. Even so *must their* wives *be* grave, not slanderers, sober, faithful in all things. Let the deacons be the husbands of one wife, ruling their children and their own houses well."

The word "deacon" means servant. In Acts 6:1-8, we learn of men being chosen to care for the physical or material needs in the congregation. "Then the twelve called the multitude of the disciples *unto them,* and said, It is not reason that we should leave the word of God, and serve tables." Though these men are not called deacons in this context, it is generally believed they were deacons. These men were not chosen to make decisions for the church, but to serve.

The preacher or evangelist has no more authority in the church than any other member. He could be a pastor only if he meets the qualifications identified in the letters to Timothy and Titus, and if he has been appointed to that office.

In the Lord's church each congregation is completely independent of all others, yet they each teach and practice the same things. This is possible only if all the congregations are going by the Bible, and only the Bible. This works, and it works well. It's happening today all over the world. So, isn't it possible for ever congregation of God's people to practice true Christianity today as they did in New Testament times?

The preacher, as usual, is wrong.

ADMISSION TO THE CHURCH AND SALVATION

Since, as we have seen, Jesus is the savior of the church, it's important that we be a part of it.

Having learned the Gospel we have to first believe if we hope to be admitted to the church. Why faith is so important is that if one doesn't believe he will not react to what he has learned. This explains why so many people learn what the Bible says then don't do what it says to do, or they argue with parts of it. They simply don't believe. If people really believed the Bible, they would jump off a cliff if it told them to. If people really believed the Bible they would not argue with the notion of being immersed in water for salvation, along with faith and other things that save us.

Why the suggestion of immersion in water? Why not sprinkle for baptism? Why do either? Why not just believe? Is faith enough?

Faith is so extremely important that without it we would not do anything the Bible tells us to. Faith is stressed through the whole New Testament. The Apostle Paul told the Romans, "So then faith *cometh* by hearing, and hearing by the word of God" (Romans 10:17). So we know that faith comes as a result of our exposure to the Bible. And Jesus said, "if ye believe not that I am *he*, ye shall die in your sins" (John 8:24). The writer of the book of Hebrews said, "But without faith *it is* impossible to please *him*: for he that cometh to God must believe that He is" (Heb. 11:6). The importance of faith cannot be over emphasized.

What about "just believe" and nothing more as the preacher says? It may sound like he's right considering what Paul said, "Therefore we conclude that a man is justified by faith without the deeds of the law" (Romans 3:28). How do you correlate this with what James said, "Ye see then how that by works a man is justified, and not by faith only" (James 2:24). The preacher must not have read the whole verse, when reading Paul's comments. Paul said we are not justified by the "works of the law." The law here is the Old Testament Law. We are not justified by obeying the Old Testament. There is no contradiction between Paul and James.

So, faith comes by hearing the Word of God, as we saw earlier. What next? It seems logical now to deal with the doctrine of "faith only." Every Sunday the preacher gets up and says that all you need to do is just believe, nothing else is necessary to save you. Just accept Jesus into your heart; that's all that's necessary, the preacher will tell you. This business of accepting Jesus into your heart is a relatively new idea. It's certainly not found in the Bible. It's true that we are saved by calling on the name of the Lord. "And it shall come to pass, *that* whosoever shall call on the name of the Lord shall be saved" (Acts 2:21). It doesn't say to just call out the name of the Lord to be saved, and it doesn't mean to just ask the Lord to save you. Calling on the name of the Lord is to do what He says to do; to act on or by His authority.

So, now, we have heard the Word of God, and we believe. Having believed, we are convicted of our sins as those people in Acts chapter two were. "Now when they heard *this,* they were pricked in their heart, and said unto Peter and to the rest of the apostles, Men *and* brethren, what shall we do?" (Acts 2:37). This is the first account of conversion found in the New Testament. Peter accused the crowd of crucifying Jesus. They were pricked in the heart, or convicted of their sin. They wanted to know what to do. What would you tell them to do? What would the preacher tell them to do? They already had heard and they believed. The preacher stops here and says that's enough. But the Apostle Peter didn't think so. The preacher is wrong! Did you know that every time in the New Testament when someone became a Christian he did the same thing Peter told that crowd to do? "Then Peter said unto them, Repent, and be baptized every one of you in the name of Jesus Christ for the remission of sins" (Acts 2:38). Whether we like it or not, whether or not it's beneath our dignity, if we are to become Christians we have to do what Peter told those people to do. If not, why not? One who argues with this is actually arguing with Peter. When did God change the rules? If man changed the rules, by whose authority did he change them? It's certainly not by God's authority.

Follow this closely: In Matt. 26:28, Jesus tells us that He shed His blood <u>for the remission of sins</u>. In Acts 2:38, Peter tells us to be baptized <u>for the remission of sins</u>, as we just read. Look at Jesus' statement: "For this is my blood of the new testament, which is shed for many for the remission of sins." The word "for" is used three times in this verse. But they each came from different words in the Greek. Why is this important? Because the preacher will tell you that we are baptized "because of" remission of sins. He's got the wrong word "for!" The preacher would have Peter saying, "repent and be baptized because of' the remission of sins." If "for" means "because of" remissions of sins here, it means that Jesus' blood was shed "because of" remission of sins in Matthew twenty-six because the same "for" (meaning in order to) is used in both places. What the preacher says is complete nonsense! Nonsense!

The first word "for" in Jesus' statement does mean "because of." It is the Greek word, "yap." The word "for" before "remission of sins" means "in order to." It is the Greek word, "eis." Now, the same word meaning "in order

111

to" (eis) is used by Peter in Acts 2:38. He was telling people to be baptized 'in order to" the remission of sins. The preacher should know that. But if he preached it, he would lose a lot of friends. (The middle "for," in Matt. 26:28, before the word "many," is defined as "concerning" or "as touching.") By the way, the American Standard Version says "unto the remission of sins."

The only time the phrase "faith only" is used in the Bible it says we are not justified by faith only. "Ye see then how that by works a man is justified, and not by faith only" (James 2:24). Those who argue that we are saved by faith only, say that we have to repent, also. So, when they say repentance is required, even they agree we are not saved by faith only. Read all of James 2:14-20. Parts are quoted here: "What *doth it* profit, my brethren, though a man say he hath faith, and have not works? can faith save him? . . . Even so faith, if it hath not works, is dead, being alone. . . . Thou believest that there is one God; thou doest well: the devils also believe, and tremble. But wilt thou know, O vain man, that faith without works is dead?"

The word "baptize" was borrowed from the original language in which the Bible was written. If it had been translated like the rest of the Bible instead of being transliterated, where we find the word "baptize" in the Bible it would say "immerse."

What are some other things the Bible says about baptism? Immediately before Jesus went back into heaven, He instructed His disciples to "Go ye into all the world, and preach the gospel to every creature. He that believeth and is baptized shall be saved; but he that believeth not shall be damned" (Mark 16:15-16). He didn't have to say he who does not be baptized shall be damned. That wasn't necessary in order to express His

112

intention.   He knew that unless they believed they wouldn't be baptized.

Can we be saved without being in Christ? As a part of Jesus' prayer in John chapter seventeen, He prayed to the Father that His followers be "one in us." "Neither pray I for these alone, but for them also which shall believe on me through their word; That they all may be one; as thou, Father, *art* in me, and I in thee, that they also may be one in us: that the world may believe that thou hast sent me" (John 17:20-21). How do we get into Christ? "For ye are all the children of God by faith in Christ Jesus. For as many of you as have been baptized into Christ have put on Christ" (Gal. 3:26-27). The only way the Bible tells us how to get into Christ is to be baptized into Christ. Notice also in this quote how important faith is, for without it we would not be children of God because we would not go on to be baptized into Christ.

There are also those sins of which we want to rid ourselves. We want to have them remitted. Peter told that crowd that had crucified Christ to "Repent, and be baptized every one of you in the name of Jesus Christ for the remission of sins" (Acts 2:38). This is the only way the Bible tells us how to have our sins remitted. The preacher can argue with this all he wants to, but it doesn't change anything.

Paul and Silas were in prison when God caused an earthquake. The prison doors were opened and the guard was about to kill himself for fear of their escape. Paul stopped him. The guard recognized something special was happening and he asked, "Sirs, what must I do to be saved?" (Acts 16:30). Paul's reply was, "Believe on the Lord Jesus Christ, and thou shalt be saved, and thy house. And they spake unto him the word of the Lord, and to all that were in his house. And he took them the same hour of the night, and washed *their* stripes; and was baptized, he and all his, straightway" (Acts 16:31-33). This explains the urgency of baptism. This guard had the kind of faith that saves. His faith caused him to go on and obey the gospel. He was baptized immediately.

There are other examples. Even Paul's own conversion demonstrates the necessity of baptism. He had been praying for three days because he believed. But he still had his sins. He was told what to do to be saved. "And now why tarriest thou? arise, and be baptized, and wash away thy sins, calling on the name of the Lord" (Acts 22:16). The preacher deals with this passage with contempt. Note, this passage also tells us something about "calling on the name of the Lord." (In I Peter. 3:21, Peter explained that it's not just washing dirt from the body.)

Paul had faith. The preacher says that's enough. He still had his sins! Surely no one could pray the "sinner's prayer" better than Paul. He prayed three days. That's what the preacher tells him to do. He still had his sins! After believing and praying for three days, Paul was told to "be baptized, and wash away thy sins." There's no such thing in the Bible as a sinner's prayer!

How could anyone argue with the instruction to be baptized? How could anyone argue that it is not essential to our salvation? The Bible plainly says that baptism saves us. Look at I Pet. 3:21: "The like figure whereunto *even* baptism doth also now save us (not the putting away of the filth of the flesh, but the answer of a good conscience toward God,) by the resurrection of Jesus Christ." The explanation in parenthesis explains that it's not washing dirt from our body. Instead, our conscience can be clear because we know that we've done what we've been instructed to do. The preacher has it wrong. He'll

114

try to explain it away. And it's important to remember that sprinkling or pouring water over someone is not baptism.

The preacher will ask about the thief on the cross. Wasn't he in paradise with Jesus? By asking this question, the preacher shows just how little he knows. He is either ignorant or dishonest. First, we don't know that the thief had not been baptized. John the baptizer had been baptizing for some time in that area. The thief could have been one of those people John had baptized. The fact is the New Testament baptism was not in effect at the time of the life and death of the thief. He lived under the Old Testament Law. Up to that point no one had been baptized with Christ's baptism. It was not until Pentecost, in Acts 2, that the apostles began baptizing people in the name of Christ. This was about fifty days after the thief died.

We know that John's baptism was different from Christ's and that John's baptism is no longer the correct baptism because of an example we find in Acts 18:24-26. There was a good man named Apollos, who "taught diligently the things of the Lord, knowing only the baptism of John." He had been baptized only by John's baptism. Some friends who heard him speak "took him unto *them*, and expounded unto him the way of God more perfectly."

Point out the necessity of baptism to the preacher and he will take you to other passages that teach that we are saved by grace or faith or whatever, thus avoiding the scriptures on baptism. Watch and see. They simply will leave the passages on baptism. No one argues that we are not saved by God's grace or by faith. Confessing Christ is important, too. The apostle Paul said, "with the mouth confession is made unto salvation" (Romans 10:9-10). So, then, we hear, we believe, we repent, we confess, and we are baptized into Christ. Once we are in Christ, we remain faithful even unto death. Jesus told the Apostle John to write to the church at Smyrna, " be thou faithful unto death, and I will give thee a crown of life" (Rev. 2:10). This suggests that if we do not remain faithful, we will not receive that crown. "Unto death" implies that we are to be faithful even if we have to die for our faith. Many have died for their faith.

Sadly, the preacher has it wrong. Chances are, the preacher himself has not been baptized into Christ. Chances are he's not been baptized for the remission of sins. This is a fair statement because he teaches that we should be baptized because of remission of sins.

The preacher has it wrong.

It's that good news, the Gospel, that moves us to even care what the preacher has to say. It's the gospel that motivates us to obey God in the first place. The Apostle Paul said, "I am not ashamed of the gospel of Christ: for it is the power of God unto salvation" (Romans 1:16).

"For God so loved the world, that he gave his only begotten Son, that whosoever believeth in him should not perish, but have everlasting life" (John 3:16).

Hundreds of years before Jesus was so unjustly slain, Isaiah gave perhaps the most touching account of what was going to take place. Here's what he had to say: "He is despised and rejected of men; a man of sorrows, and acquainted with grief: . . . he was despised, and we esteemed him not. Surely he hath borne our griefs, and carried our sorrows: . . . But he *was* wounded for our transgressions, *he was* bruised for our iniquities: ...with his stripes we are healed. All we like sheep have gone astray; we have turned everyone to his own way; and the Lord hath laid on him the iniquity of us all. He was oppressed, and he was afflicted, yet he opened not his mouth: he is brought as a lamb to the slaughter, and as a sheep before her shearers is dumb, so he openeth not his mouth. . . . Yet it pleased the Lord to bruise him; he hath put *him* to grief: when thou shalt make his soul an offering for sin, . . ." (Isaiah 53:3-12).

Jesus was despised, rejected, wounded, bruised, afflicted and oppressed, all of this for us. He was a man of sorrows. He experienced grief. He was beaten with stripes. He endured this because of our sins. He was led like a sheep to be sheared or a lamb for slaughter.

"Then did they spit in his face, and buffeted him; and others smote *him* with the palms of their hands" (Matt. 26:67). "And when they had platted a crown of thorns, they put *it* upon his head, and a reed in his right hand: and they bowed the knee before him, and mocked him, saying, Hail, King of the Jews! And they spit upon him, and took the reed, and smote him on the head. And after that they had mocked him, they took the robe off from him, and put his own raiment on him, and led him away to crucify *him*" (Matt. 27:29-31). Jesus endured this willingly.

Jesus knew what awaited Him in Jerusalem. But He went anyway. Most of us would have gone the other way as fast as possible! As He and His disciples were on their way to Jerusalem, Jesus spoke to them saying, "Behold, we go up to Jerusalem; and the Son of man shall be delivered unto the chief priests, and unto the scribes; and they shall condemn him to death, and shall deliver him to the Gentiles: And they shall mock him, and shall scourge him, and shall spit upon him, and shall kill him: and the third day he shall rise again" (Mark 10:33-34).

Just one of these things that happened to Jesus is bad enough. Spit onto your neighbor's face and see what he does. Any one of these malicious deeds would be enough to provoke most of us to fight. How do you react when someone deliberately drives a nail through your hand? How do you feel when someone ridicules you? What is it like to have a branch with thorns wrapped around your head, or to be struck across the head with a reed? If one deserved all this it would still make him want to fight back. Of course, we know that Jesus deserved none of this and that He didn't resist.

The Roman soldiers enjoyed punishing Jesus. The Bible doesn't say that, but they had to be enjoying it to do what they did. With eyes closed it's easy to see these brutes mocking Him and having their fun for the day. The punks! But wait! We were all in Jerusalem that day. Just where in Jerusalem were we?

Each must ask the question: "Where was I in the crowd that day?" "Did I cry out "crucify!?" "Was I the scribe, one who should have known the Old Testament teachings regarding the coming of Christ, yet I condemned Him?" "Was I the one who drove the first nail into His hand?" All the masses of humanity were there that day. It's no wonder the sky turned dark!

Jesus was betrayed by one of His disciples. His friends ran when He was captured. One cursed and denied Him. He was bound. His face was spit upon. He was struck, and mocked. He was reviled. False accusations were made against Him. He was derided, and a crown of thorns was placed upon Him. The chief priest, who should have recognized Him as the Messiah, said, "we have no king but Caesar." As much as they hated Caesar, they chose him over Jesus. They must have really hated Jesus. The mob preferred a criminal to Jesus. He did no evil and as He was dying He said, "Father forgive them", and to the Father, "why hast thou forsaken me?" A soldier pierced His side to make sure He was dead. How could any of us reject one who was spit on, slapped about and crucified for us?

We all put Him to death!

"God commendeth his love toward us, in that, while we were yet sinners, Christ died for us" (Romans 5:8). But it is possible to figuratively crucify Him all over again. Speaking of Christians, the writer of the book of Hebrews said, "If they shall fall away. . . seeing they crucify to

119

themselves the Son of God afresh, and put *him* to an open shame" (Heb. 6:6).

Though we crucified Him, Jesus invites all of mankind to come to Him to be saved. "Come unto me, all *ye* that labour and are heavy laden, and I will give you rest" (Matt. 11:28). That's the very purpose for which he came. "For the Son of man is come to save that which was lost" (Matt. 18:11). The Apostle Peter said, "Forasmuch as ye know that ye were not redeemed with corruptible things, *as* silver and gold, . . But with the precious blood of Christ, as of a lamb without blemish and without spot" (1 Peter 1:18-19). How do we compare His blood to silver and gold? Gold is worthless when we consider the question posed by the writer of Hebrews: "How shall we escape, if we neglect so great salvation?" (Heb. 2:3).

Each of us should ask, "How grateful am I?" It comes down to what may be an even more profound question: "Do I believe, do I really believe all this happened?" If not, it would behoove us to start studying to determine if this is something we should believe. One believing his house is burning would do anything to get out. One believing his house is burning would give anything to get out. Since most of us do nearly nothing to avoid a burning hell, surely most of us don't really believe!

Back to the question, "How grateful am I?" The Psalmist said, "I have longed for thy salvation, O Lord; and thy law *is* my delight" (Psalms 119:174), and "Restore unto me the joy of thy salvation; and uphold me *with thy* free spirit" (Psalms 51:12).

Who is brave enough to ignore the offer of salvation by his creator and to reject the benefit of the crucifixion of His Son? The time will come "That at the name of Jesus every knee should bow, . . . And every tongue should

120

confess that Jesus Christ *is* Lord, to the glory of God the Father" (Phil. 2:-10-11). "So then every one of us shall give account of himself to God" (Romans 14:12). "For the great day of His wrath is come; and who shall be able to stand?" (Rev. 6:17). "How shall we escape, if we neglect so great salvation . . . ." (Heb. 2:3).

"Seek ye the Lord while he may be found, call ye upon him while he is near: Let the wicked forsake his way, and the unrighteous man his thoughts: and let him return unto the LORD, and he will have mercy upon him; and to our God, for he will abundantly pardon" (Isaiah 55:6-7).

Some people are embarrassed to acknowledge belief in the gospel. Pity the man who is ashamed of the gospel! It leads us to salvation. "For I am not ashamed of the gospel of Christ: for it is the power of God unto salvation" (Romans 1:16). Ponder the excitement and the euphoria we should experience upon learning and obeying the gospel of Christ, knowing our sins are forgiven and we are on our way to heaven, and knowing that God will hear our prayers.

When we are in God's hands all is well. There's nothing to worry about; all is well now and all will be well when the end comes. Paul said, "Be careful for nothing; but in every thing by prayer and supplication with thanksgiving let your requests be made known unto God. And the peace of God, which passeth all understanding, shall keep your hearts and minds through Christ Jesus" (Phil. 4:6-7). Since we "all have sinned, and come short of the glory of God" (Romans 3:23), we all need the redemption that comes through Christ.

God's Word will not return to Him void, it shall accomplish its purpose and "it shall prosper *in the thing* whereto I sent it. For ye shall go out with joy, and be led

121

forth with peace: the mountains and the hills shall break forth before you into singing, and all the trees of the field shall clap *their* hands" (Isaiah 55:10-13).

Imagine the excitement, trees clapping their hands and hills breaking forth in song! "The Lord *is* my shepherd; I shall not want" (Psalms 23:1). "The Lord shall preserve thee from all evil: he shall preserve thy soul" (Psalms 121:7).

What an awesome gift! How different would we feel if we learned that just yesterday a friend died for us? In fact, we learn that he was tortured before he was killed. What would we do for that person? Of course, nothing now since he is dead; but not so with Christ. He lives again!

And He said, "if ye love me keep my commandments."

"Sing unto the Lord, all the earth; shew forth from day to day his salvation" (1 Chron. 16:23).

Is your choice to serve the Lord and be saved, or will you hold onto the traditions of men, and take a chance with your soul?

For information about how to find people who hold to the views expressed in this book contact Ed Smith at:

coonties@ymail.com

508 Pool Branch Road
Fort Meade, Florida, 33841
USA

www.ingramcontent.com/pod-product-compliance
Lightning Source LLC
Chambersburg PA
CBHW060515030426
42337CB00015B/1903